Other works by Dr. Darlington Ndubuike

"Multicultural Education in Urban Schools," in *Problems and Solutions in Urban Schools*, edited by Gwendolyn M. Duhon (2001)

The Struggles, Challenges, and Triumphs of the African Immigrants in America (2002)

I Too Dream America (2004)

UNLEASH YOUR POTENTIAL

Put Any Foot Forward

Dr. Darlington I. I. Ndubuike

iUniverse LLC
Bloomington

UNLEASH YOUR POTENTIAL
PUT ANY FOOT FORWARD

iUniverse books may be ordered through booksellers or by contacting:

iUniverse
1663 Liberty Drive
Bloomington, IN 47403
www.iuniverse.com
1-800-Authors (1-800-288-4677)

Because of the dynamic nature of the Internet, any web addresses or links contained in this book may have changed since publication and may no longer be valid. The views expressed in this work are solely those of the author and do not necessarily reflect the views of the publisher, and the publisher hereby disclaims any responsibility for them.

Any people depicted in stock imagery provided by Thinkstock are models, and such images are being used for illustrative purposes only. Certain stock imagery © Thinkstock.

Scripture taken from the King James Version of the Bible.

ISBN: 978-1-4917-2987-8 (sc)
ISBN: 978-1-4917-2988-5 (hc)
ISBN: 978-1-4917-2989-2 (e)

Library of Congress Control Number: 2014905329

Printed in the United States of America.

iUniverse rev. date: 04/25/2014

To my wife, Patience, for faithfully walking
alongside me every step of the way,
and
my children, Valentine, Candice, Leslie, and Valerie,

as we, together, unleash our potential.

Contents

Preface

This book came as a result of prayer. I have always had in mind to write a sequel to my previous book, *I Too Dream America*, but time had not permitted me to do so. As an adult Christian education teacher at my church, I was studying a book by John Ortberg, *If You Want to Walk on Water, You've Got to Get Out of the Boat*. In one of the chapters, I came across a section where the author gave a six-month prayer challenge. He told a story of how he encouraged someone to pray for six months for something specific that he wanted God to do for him. Before the six-month period expired, the man received an answer to his prayers. John Ortberg challenged anyone reading the book to take him up on that six-month challenge, offering to give full refund of the cost of the book if the prayer went unanswered.

After the lesson that day, I presented that challenge to the entire Sunday school class, and we all agreed to participate in the six-month prayer challenge. We didn't get into it to prove Mr. Ortberg wrong; we didn't get into it so that we would get our money back if it failed; we didn't get into it to try God; we all decided to get into it to seize the opportunity.

I was specific in my prayer; well, as specific as I could be. My prayer throughout the period was for God to take me to a new level, to expand my territory. I honestly didn't know which level I wanted Him to take me to. I couldn't tell Him which territory I wanted Him to expand. But I prayed that prayer and held on tightly by faith.

Then, about a month into this experience, I began to feel an overwhelming urge to write. I have written and published other books before now, but the direction that this particular one was leading me in was different, a terrain I have never explored. It continued to unfold as I progressed; somehow the well opened, and the river began to flow: fresh water of ideas, a synthesis of personal experience untrammeled by prior knowledge and background. I would get up in the middle of the night to jot down ideas that came to mind. I would pull over to the side of the road to write. I would interrupt dinner because an idea was floating in my mind.

How it all came together was only God's doing, and it is marvelous in my sight. It was interesting that the inspiration for this book came directly from John Ortberg's book. My prayers turned out to fulfill my desire to write a sequel to my previous book.

This book is a clarion call for us to stir up the gifts inside us. Everyone has a gift, and there is urgency for us all to use the gifts we have been given as God has purposed them. The truth is that if we don't use our gifts, we will lose the joy of fulfilling God's purpose in our lives. God dares us to unleash our potential. This book is a call of motivation and encouragement to put a foot forward, any foot, especially when we have to surf unknown waters.

We must arise, take up our beds, and walk. We may have been crippled for so long by our circumstances, our fears, our trepidations and all, but we are encouraged to heed the command of the Lord to arise! We see how our shoes can hinder our ability to put a foot forward. We are encouraged to take off those shoes so that we can take that step. We can prepare ourselves to face whatever assignments we are given and whatever challenges we may confront in the process, armed with the understanding of who we are and the gifts of God in us.

When God brings opportunities our way, and when we can ascertain that it is God doing so, then we have to take that STEP:

- Seize the opportunity
- Take action by faith
- Encourage ourselves in the Lord
- Prayerfully follow God's lead

We cannot be intimidated by our circumstances. We must hold our heads up and keep our shoulders high. No one should have to be alone in the struggles of life. We need each other to unleash our potential.

Once we are able to understand and utilize the contents of our BACKPACK—background, ability, cultural orientation, knowledge, personality, attitude, communication pattern, and keep—it stirs us to the right direction. It is the knowledge of the contents of our BACKPACK that will facilitate our decision to take the step. We must position ourselves to unleash our potential without losing focus. We must understand that nothing good comes easy. It takes a process, but the dream is attainable. It takes determination, acceptance of challenge, readiness to perform, and enthusiasm. It takes preparation, understanding of who we are, self-determination, and honesty. It takes commitment and our ability to make the right choices.

Chapter 1 calls us to stir up the gifts in us. It's a call for you and me and everyone to use the gifts we have been given as God has purposed them. It calls us to identify our gifts and begin to put them in good use.

Chapter 2 dares us to unleash our potential. It is a call of motivation and encouragement. We must find an intrinsic motivation to put a foot forward, especially when we have to surf unknown waters.

In chapter 3, we are commanded to arise, take up our beds, and walk. We may have been crippled by our circumstances and our fears, but we are encouraged to heed the command of the Lord.

In chapter 4, we see how our shoes can hinder our ability to put a foot forward. We are encouraged to take off those shoes so that we can take that step.

Chapter 5 calls us to prepare ourselves to face whatever assignments we are given and whatever challenges we may confront in the process. It is an encouragement for us to understand who we are and the gifts of God in us.

Chapter 6 calls us to know when God brings opportunities our way. Once we can ascertain that an opportunity is from God, then we have to take that STEP: seize the opportunity, take action by faith, encourage ourselves in the Lord, and prayerfully follow God's lead.

Chapter 7 speaks on the use of our CASH: charisma, attitude, skill, and honesty. We must not be intimidated by our circumstances. We must hold our heads up and keep our shoulders high.

Chapter 8 speaks of the need to connect with others. No one should have to be alone in the struggles of life. We need each other to unleash our potential.

Chapter 9 discusses how to understand and utilize the contents of our BACKPACK. It is this knowledge that will facilitate our decision to take the step.

Chapter 10 calls to our attention the need to stay focused. The *fruits* are essential for healthy choices.

Chapter 11 encourages us to unlock our PADLOCK: to position ourselves, make the necessary adjustments, deal with our fears, locate our opportunities, remain optimistic, cultivate our gifts, and keep open minds.

Finally, in chapter 12, we see that nothing good comes easy; it takes a process. I discuss my experiences and journey to the fulfillment of my dreams. It comes as a sequel to *I Too Dream America*.

I feel blessed to be used by God in this way. I have gained more understanding of the ways of God. He is the Potter, and if we allow Him, He will mold us for His own good use.

Don't put it off any longer. I DARE you to PUSH yourself. Utilize your CASH. Take that STEP. Unlock that PADLOCK. Stir up that gift in you. Go ahead; unleash your potential. Put a foot forward—any foot!

—Dr. D.

Acknowledgments

My sincere gratitude goes to Mr. Lawrence Ukpabi Nwagbara, Mr. and Mrs. Ebi and Mina Komonibo, and the *Drum Magazine*, Houston, who took their time and meticulously read the entire manuscript.

I appreciate all the members of the Light Bearer's class at the Braeswood Assembly of God Church in Houston, Texas, for their support and encouragement.

I want to thank my senior pastor and his wife, Steve and Donna Banning, for their unconditional love, and Pastor Donnie Mooney for giving me the opportunity to unleash my potential.

1

Stir Up the Gift in You

Almost everyone I know who has reached some level of success also has a story of obstacles and even failure. Success, therefore, is not attained by a sudden flight. It is by falling and rising again that one attains real success. Success eludes us only when we fall and refuse to rise. Failure and obstacles must come, but the gifts in us must motivate us to arise and put any foot forward. We know from the Scriptures that a man's gift makes way for him (Proverbs 18:16), and we are encouraged to stir up the gifts in us (2 Timothy 1:6).

We have all received gifts at one point or another in our lives. In our world today, many opportunities arise throughout the year for gift-giving. In February, we have Valentine's Day. In May, we celebrate Mother's Day. In June, Father's Day comes around, then Thanksgiving in November and Christmas in December. These are in addition to birthdays and anniversaries and other special occasions.

Gifts are given to be used. Unless we use our gifts, they have no practical value. Perishable gifts, if not used, decay and rot away. Other types of gifts, if not used, just sit and collect dust. Sometimes we think that gifts are too good to be used, and we "preserve" them. We rent a storage space and put them away in there, and we end up paying more for the storage space than the gift itself is worth. We tend to forget that the giver expects the recipient to use the gift. Sometimes we return our gifts to the store for refunds, exchanges, or alterations, depending on the type of gift. Some of us practice regifting: rewrapping our gift and giving it to someone else.

I was reading John Ortberg's story about how his grandmother stowed away precious chinaware that had been given to her, waiting for a special occasion when she would use it. That special occasion never came, and she died. That precious gift stayed wrapped up carefully, packed in a box and stowed in the attic.

At one point or another in our lives, we all have been given gifts that we have put away for a special occasion, an occasion that may never take place.

One Father's Day, my daughter gave me the gift of a tie. Considering that she was in college then and wasn't making any money, I cherished that tie even more. I kept the tie in my closet, waiting for a special occasion to wear it. I didn't know what special occasion I was waiting for. I didn't have any event in mind. That "special occasion" didn't come around, and that tie hung in my closet for a long time with the tag still on it.

What I didn't realize was that my daughter was waiting to see me wear that tie. It was a special gift from daughter to Daddy, and I should have known that.

One Sunday, I dressed up and put on that tie. When my daughter saw me, the very first thing she said was, "About time, Daddy!" She didn't think I cherished the tie or appreciated the gift. She had every right to believe so. There was no way for her to know how I felt unless I showed it by wearing the tie. Instead, I had buried the gift. I felt so bad!

I received many compliments about that tie all day at church. Even when we stopped to eat at a restaurant, compliments poured like rain. My daughter beamed with satisfaction. She wasn't just happy that I wore the tie and received compliments; she was also proud that she made the right choice of gift for her dad.

There was no way I could have known that the tie was so great if I hadn't worn it. My daughter's facial expression was priceless, and that feeling wouldn't have come alive if I hadn't worn the tie. The tie had such potential, and that potential wouldn't have manifested if it hadn't been unleashed by my action. Not to mention that I got some more ties after that!

I don't know what other gifts I have buried, knowingly or unknowingly. Gifts are given, not only to be appreciated, but to be put to good use. Again, the giver of the gift expects the recipient to use the gift. There may be countless gifts collecting dust today, buried in the closet or in the attic or under the bed or in the garage, and unless those gifts are brought out and put to use, they will just sit there and rust.

Everyone given a gift must account for the gift. On the day that I wore the tie my daughter gave me, part of her reaction was, "Daddy, I was about to ask you what you did with the tie I gave you for Father's Day, because I haven't seen you wear it." That hurts, doesn't it? A gift is given not just to benefit you, but also to benefit others.

Our God, the Master Gift Giver, gives gifts that are tailored to perfection. Every one of us has received unique gifts from the Master, and these gifts are not transferable, alterable, or exchangeable. Either you use your gift or you forfeit it entirely. Our gifts should create avenues for us. Such gifts should make the recipient rich and should come with no sorrow.

Jesus demonstrates this concept in the parable of the talents (Matthew 25:14–30). You know the story. Jesus told of a certain man who gave his three servants talents before he traveled. To one servant, he gave five talents; to the second, he gave two talents; and to the third, he gave one talent.

I want you to know right away that the issue is not about the number of talents given. The Master knows each person's ability, and He would not give anyone something he could not handle. Recall in verse 15 it says, "To every man according to his ability." Therefore, the Gift Giver knows our individual abilities, and He gives based on our capability. It doesn't matter how many talents you have received; what counts is what you do with what you have received.

Notice the response of the master as each servant came to account for the gift he had received. The master said to the servant who received five talents, "Well done, thou good and faithful servant; thou hast been faithful over a few things, I will make thee ruler over many things; enter thou into the joy of thy lord" (verse 21). Then the second servant came and gave account of his stewardship, and the master said the same thing to him verbatim: "Well done, thou good and faithful servant; thou hast been faithful over a few things, I will make thee ruler over many things; enter thou into the joy of thy lord" (verse 23).

Both servants received the same reward regardless of the number of talents they had been given. Hence, it is not about whether you are a five-talent person or a two-talent person; the rewards are the same. To those who did something with what they had been given, more was given. They were promoted, elevated. The master said to them, "Thou hast been faithful over a few things, I will make thee ruler over many things. Enter into the joy of your master" (verses 21 and 23).

So you see, when you unleash your potential, when you put a foot forward, any foot, you will find that more avenues will open. Better opportunities will come your way. All you have to do is make a move. Put any foot forward. Take that step!

After completing my undergraduate degree, I began teaching at an elementary school. I had been told that I would not get a job as a teacher in the United States of America because of my accent. I knew teaching was my passion, and I was devastated to hear from my friends that I would not be able to teach. I made a decision to put my foot forward. I applied to teach at an inner-city elementary school, and I got the job. Other doors opened—better doors.

On the other hand, those whose gifts are dormant and unutilized live lives of stagnation, dejection, and emptiness. There is nothing as painful as a buried talent. The tragedy of it all is that the talent you had, if not put in use, will be taken from you and given to someone who is making use of his talent. The third servant was harshly rebuked for failure to unleash his potential, for failure to put a foot forward. He didn't even try. Nothing was mentioned in the rebuke about the number of talents he had been given, but a lot was said about lack of use. The issue was about potential not unleashed, the refusal to put a foot forward—any foot! The third servant had many excuses. Unfortunately excuses will not exonerate us when we fail to act.

When I was considering writing this book, I battled with many thoughts: *Am I qualified to write on this topic? Will I have time to complete it? Will it turn out the way I envision it?* I thought about the many would-be obstacles: workload, church activities, family concerns, community obligations, and on and on. I made the decision to put my foot forward. I did, and the rest is history.

If I hadn't started, I wouldn't have experienced the thrill of completion. You wouldn't be reading this book right now. I would have ended up burying my gift and would have risked standing face-to-face with the Father of all gifts to account for the buried talent.

Have you heard someone tell you that you have the potential to become a great leader, attorney, teacher, doctor, preacher, or any other "gifted" role? Potential is just what it is—potential. If nothing is done about it, it is dead. There are many potentials walking around today in disuse. Some are interred in the grave because no one unleashed them. Potential is like faith: without works (that is, if not unleashed), faith is dead!

I have seen many inmates who never knew they had talents until they went to jail. They discovered that they had buried the most precious gifts of their lives all these years. Some had artistic talents and produced the most beautiful artworks ever imagined. Some discovered that they had great voices and produced the most beautiful music ever heard. I have always wondered what their situations might have been if they had taken the time to discover these wonderful gifts while they were free.

A family friend graduated from nursing school and became licensed as a registered nurse. She could have settled for working in a hospital setting, where she would be guaranteed regular paychecks. At least she would make enough to pay her mortgage, car note, and other bills.

But she knew there was a gift she needed to stir up. Going back to get her certification as a family nurse practitioner (FNP) would come with a price. She would lose the opportunity to make money during her period of additional study, running the risks of not taking "good" care of her family and perhaps of losing some inherent benefits. The FNP program was not an easy choice, but she decided to accept the challenge and put a foot forward. She took the risk, knowing that she might face a storm along the way.

Guess what? She completed the FNP program. Again, she could have settled for the "big pay" of working in the hospital or in a doctor's office. But again, she decided to put a foot forward. She opened her own clinic. She knew there would be a storm. Where would the patients come from? Where would the money come from? How about the hassle of setting up a clinic? She faced all of these questions and more. But she decided to unleash her potential. She was ready to face the storm. And she did. She opened her own pediatric clinic.

Then recently, someone moved out of an office space adjacent to hers. She saw it as an opportunity to grow—perhaps the chance of a lifetime to open her gift. She had a beautiful home. She had beautiful children. She had a wonderful husband. She didn't need to "stress" herself any further.

She must have inquired of the Lord, "Shall I go forth?"

She must have heard a voice that said, "Go forth!"

Then she must have asked, "Jesus, is it you?"

Jesus would have said to her, "It is I. Do not be afraid!"

She must have said, "Lord, if it is you, command me to unleash my potential."

Jesus would have said to her, "Unleash! I have given you that gift; open it!"

My friend was terrified. She saw the storm wind coming again. How would she pay for this extra space? Where would she get the patients to sustain the larger practice? What if?

Again, she ignored the storm and put a foot forward. Expansion of the office space was completed. She moved in. She realized that this was the opportunity of a lifetime. She had minimized the gap between what shall be and what might have been—you know, the regret factor at the end of life!

You don't have to see all the benefits before you put a foot forward. There may have been eleven other RNs and FNPs who refused to take the risk of putting a foot forward.

What about you? Do you have a gift you have not yet discovered? Not everyone can be a doctor or lawyer or engineer or teacher. There is a different special gift for each of us. I have a friend named Ricky who is a handyman. He did not go to school for it. He has not received a degree in structural engineering or architectural design. But he is the most brilliant handyman I have ever met. There is nothing he cannot fix in your home. There is nothing he cannot build. I bet that when he started his business, people mocked him. "How can he have earned a degree, yet ended up fixing drains and toilets?" But look at him now!

I am a five-talent kind of guy. I am in continuous prayer every day, asking God to help me unleash those talents. I have to put my foot forward at any opportunity I get to do so. I can't sit there and allow fear to cripple me; if I did, it would be as if I were sitting by the pool of Bethesda and watching others jump into the water to make their lives better. I would have to give an account of what I had done with the gifts God gave me.

Do you have gifts that you know you have not used? Is there a burning passion you know you have not explored, perhaps due to fear or doubt or skepticism or trepidation or past failures? Recall that Peter spent a whole day casting his net into the lake and caught nothing. But when Jesus came, He asked Peter to cast his net again into the same lake. Peter did, and he achieved success.

You might have tried previously and failed. You might have been criticized, booed, and ridiculed. I dare you to put a foot forward today. I dare you to unleash your potential today. Don't let it linger. Take that step.

2

DARE to Unleash
Your Potential

Determination

Whatever you have chosen to do, do it well. You know that you have a job to do. You are determined to do it and to do it to the best of your ability. You are dedicated and committed. You have set your mind to accomplish a goal. Your passion for your chosen career must be the drive to that end.

Don't go to school merely because others are going. Don't go because you want to please your parents, your spouse, or your family. Go because you want to go.

You will never discover your gift until you put a foot forward. There are many who don't have the opportunity to be where you are or to do what you are doing. They are fervently praying for opportunity to arise. It does not matter where you are at this point. What matters is your willingness to put a foot forward.

I watched as the season 12 *American Idol* winner, Candice Glover, took her crown on television. Her road to fame was rough, bumpy, and rugged, with several detours, but she was determined to let that little light of hers shine, and shine it did. She was on the audition stage for three years, and she faced rejections, but she was determined to unleash her potential. All she did was cast her net again in the same lake. She put a foot forward, and then she was walking on water. It was her determination to use her gift that propelled her to great heights.

Again, she did not get there by a sudden flight. What if she had bailed out after the first rejection or the second? Then she would have buried her precious gift. I wonder how many contestants left in anger or frustration or simple dejection and refused to try again. They knew they had the gift; what they lacked was the determination to persevere.

There was a woman with an issue of blood (Matthew 9:20–22). We can imagine her as a lady, perhaps frail. She wanted badly to unleash her potential. She wanted badly to have a better life. She knew that where she was was not where she was supposed to be. She desperately wanted to touch Jesus. It was the opportunity of a lifetime for her, and she wouldn't have missed it for anything in the world. She put a foot forward toward Jesus. With determination, she pushed through the crowd, stretching her hand as far as she could. She must have been knocked down many times. She must have been gasping for breath, but she held on. She could have given up when she was knocked down, perhaps more than once, perhaps more than twice.

Falling down is not defeat; staying down is. Many boxers have been knocked to the canvas, but they have gotten up to defeat their opponents. Mike Tyson knocked down Buster Douglas first during their history-making fight. Douglas did not stay down; he got up and defeated the world champion.

The little, frail lady got up and pushed on. Then something happened. She touched Jesus, and her life changed. What a feeling!

I know someone who applied for admission to a particular college to pursue a particular degree. Over and over again, he was refused admission. His parents asked him to pursue another major and get it over with, or apply to another college somewhere else, but he insisted that he wanted to stay with his passion. Having completed all the relevant electives at a junior college, he continued to take other classes while waiting to gain admission to his desired college in his desired major.

After several years of repeated applications, nonrefundable application fees, and rejections, he decided to cast his net again into the deep for a catch. He put another foot forward, and something happened.

He received a letter of admission, not just into the college of his choice, but also into the major of his choice. It took determination.

In Mark 10:46–52, we read an account of a blind man who heard that Jesus of Nazareth was passing by his neck of the woods. What an opportunity—the opportunity of a lifetime—and he didn't want that to pass him by. He didn't see Jesus, because he was blind, but he heard the noise.

Sometimes we are blinded by our unbelief, laziness, doubt, rejections, or fear. Maybe someone has told us in the past, "You will not amount to anything," or "You aren't going anywhere." But an opportunity comes. We don't have to see it; all we have to do is embrace it. Put a foot forward—any foot!

On this fateful day, there were a great number of people, and the noise was deafening. Yet that didn't deter the determined blind man. He continued to call out to his Destiny Changer. Even when he was rebuked, that motivated him to shout louder. Candice Glover stated that when she read the criticisms written by people on the Internet, their comments encouraged her to strive even harder. The blind man did the same—he kept on striving harder. He cried out even louder. The more he was rebuked, the louder his voice.

Then something happened. Jesus stood still. Jesus commanded the blind man to be called. Then it was those who had wanted to silence the blind man who went to bring him to Jesus. The blind man's life changed.

Jesus Himself taught persistent determination. In Luke 18:1–8, He told of a widow who would not give up. Despite the judge's refusal to grant her request, she continued to bother him. Eventually, the judge succumbed. You can't give up when you have tried and failed. You can't give up because you were turned down the first time or rejected by someone.

In high school, Michael Jordan did not make his varsity basketball team. Instead of throwing in the towel and burying his gift, he decided to use that rejection as a motivating force to unleash his potential. He put a foot forward, and then something happened: he became the best player to ever play the game of basketball. (That's my own estimation.)

In the history of the United States of America, no black person occupied the White House as president before Barack Obama came into the picture. This young man knew what he was up against and was determined to make a difference, to rewrite history. This was a child whose parents had little in terms of money. This was a boy who knew what struggles were. None of these stopped him. He realized the essence of hard work. He had a dream. He put a foot forward against criticisms and negativism. Then something happened—he became the first black president of the great United States of America.

Oprah Winfrey did not find herself in everybody's living room overnight. Her road to stardom was bumpy, with many detours. She was born into poverty and went through difficult times, but those ordeals did not stop her. She had a unique gift, and she was determined to unleash it. She put a foot forward, and something happened—she became the wealthiest black female of her time.

The pastor of Lakewood Church, Joel Osteen, worked behind the scenes when his father was pastor of the church. When his father died, the mantle fell on Joel. He must have felt a huge pressure to "fill those shoes," as he said, to honor his father. He didn't know if he was ready to be the pastor of America's largest church, but he determined that it was up to him to make a difference. It was the opportunity of a lifetime, and he didn't want to let it pass him by. He put a foot forward. Then something happened—he discovered that he was a five-talent kind of guy. Joel is an author, speaker, pastor, preacher, comedian, and perhaps much more. If he had rejected that divine offer, if he had not picked up the mantle, if he had missed that opportunity of a lifetime, he would have had to give an account to God of many buried talents.

As a little girl in high school, the last thing my wife wanted to become was a nurse. When she was selecting the subjects she would concentrate on for her West African School Certificate exams in Nigeria, she made sure that nothing would stir her toward nursing. She loved broadcast journalism, and that was what she wanted to become—a journalist.

When she came to the United States, she enrolled in a junior college and began working part-time at a restaurant. She came home after the first day at work and told me she wanted to major in nursing. I thought she was out of her mind. Before I knew it, she had changed her major.

Two years and a son later, she received her associate's degree in nursing. She developed such passion for nursing that nothing else mattered. She would tell me that she wasn't just a nurse, but also her patients' advocate. She came to my college graduation and determined that she must go to a four-year college to earn her bachelor of science degree in nursing. She achieved it.

All my wife did was put a foot forward. What fascinated me was her determination to succeed against all odds. She knew it wasn't going to be easy, but she unleashed anyway. She would stay up all night studying because she had a lot of catching up to do. She would take a quick nap and rush off to her full-time job. She was doing all that while at the same time raising her babies.

Determination to succeed comes with a price, but you must accept the challenges.

Acceptance of challenge

You know by now that there is a challenge ahead of you, and you are determined to make a difference by accepting the challenge. If you are a teacher, your mountain could be the challenges of teaching students whose cultural, ethnic, racial, and linguistic backgrounds differ from yours. Your students have different values, make different choices, and operate from different cultural scripts. You may not have all the materials you need. You may not have all the support you need. You may not have all the respect you deserve. But you have *you*, because you have accepted the challenge.

If you are a student, the giant hindering your way might be those friends who want you to go out to a party when you know you have major exams to take. Understand that you are doing what you are doing today because you have accepted the challenge.

It has always been said that nothing good comes easy. If we must get to the mountaintop, we must be ready to climb the steep slope. Peter saw the wind was boisterous (Matthew 14:22–36). He knew that no human being had ever walked on water, but he put a foot forward and became the first human to accomplish that feat. There were others with him on that day. They simply sat and watched. They were terrified by the challenges ahead. They were deterred and intimidated by the obstacles they saw. They failed to accept the challenge, and consequently the thrill that Peter experienced eluded them.

Joseph knew quite well that his brothers hated him, but he went looking for them in the wilderness to give them food. Some of us would stay away from such wicked family members. Joseph even got lost in the wilderness (Genesis 37:15–17). Some of us would have given up. Getting lost is a good excuse, but Joseph persisted. He put a foot forward, and eventually a caravan lifted him to where he unleashed his potential.

Martin Luther King Jr. went on the mountaintop. He saw the Promised Land and the challenges and obstacles on the way to it, yet that didn't intimidate him. He was knocked down several times, yet he got up and continued the fight for freedom. He put a foot forward, and then something happened—his dream became the American dream.

Challenges abound in all areas of life. Obtaining a degree comes with challenges. Securing a new job comes with new challenges. Promotion comes with unknown challenges. Either you accept the challenges and put a foot forward, or you sit where you are, bury your gift, and allow life to pass you by. People may tell you that you can't do it, but if you allow yourself to succumb to the foolish counsel of Ahithophel, you may never experience victory.

I was told by those who came before me that I would not get a job as a teacher in America because some of them had tried it and failed. They reasoned that too many things militated against me—my accent, my national origin, and my gender, because there were few male teachers. I saw the challenges, yet I put my foot forward. Then something happened—I experienced the thrill of a successful career in education in America.

You remember the 2013 *American Idol* winner we saw earlier? The challenges were unspeakable, but Candice accepted them. She continued to persevere against all odds. The taunting words of the judges, the criticisms of people on the Internet, and the pressure of singing in front of a huge audience did not stop her. In fact, they fueled her desire to attain the crown. Often we shy away from criticism when we attempt to put a foot forward. Often we are willing to bury our talents rather than resist the pressure and face the storm.

You remember the little old lady who wanted to touch the hem of Jesus's garment? Many times she must have been pushed down by the stronger crowd. She knew her life would change if only she could get close. She saw the storm, the obstacle, the distance she would have to go, the crowd she would have to overcome. She accepted the challenge because she was determined to be made well—to make her life better.

She must have been pushed down several times. She didn't stay down. She got up and pressed on. Her eyes were on the prize. She accepted the challenge.

You remember Buster Douglas? Before his fight against Iron Mike Tyson, he had some challenges to overcome. His mother had died just few weeks before, and his son's mother was seriously ill. But Douglas was determined to make his mark, and he did not allow those challenges to distort his focus. Douglas knew he was about to engage in a battle of his life. He was up against the undefeated world champion, one who had a history of devastating knockout punches. Douglas was not intimidated. He accepted the challenge and faced the storm head-on. He put a foot forward. Then something happened—he pulled off one of the biggest upsets in boxing history. He defeated the undefeated heavyweight champion of the world. What a feeling!

My wife can tell you more of her experiences also. She had children to raise at the same time she was working on her nursing degree. There were other bills to pay, including foreign-student tuition rates. She had to work full-time and study full-time. There were only twenty-four hours in a day. All these circumstances pressed her down, but she refused to stay down. She pushed on because she had her eyes on the prize. Then something happened—she walked on water! She received her nursing degree.

What about you? There is something that you have always wanted to achieve, but you have seen the storm of challenges ahead. Perhaps you are becoming weary and are about to throw in the towel. Start by putting a foot forward, any foot, and accepting the challenges. It is by accepting the challenges that you are able to face them. Once you are determined and accept the challenges, then you are ready to perform.

Readiness to perform

You are determined, and you accept the challenge. Now you are ready to put your foot forward. It is time to unleash your potential.

When you get into the exam hall and you know you have prepared for the exam, the feeling is different. The determination to pass this exam and the awareness and acceptance of the challenges that go with it elicit confidence and peace of mind. Permit me to go back for just a minute to Buster Douglas. He was determined to win the title of world boxing champion. He saw the giant in his way, ready to hinder, but he accepted the challenge to battle. Because he worked hard and prepared himself well, he was ready to perform.

Readiness involves physical and mental alertness. Once you have determined to unleash your potential and have accepted the challenges even before you face them, your body and mind are ready to absorb the punches. Again, it does not mean that you will not be knocked down, but you will not stay down.

American football, for example, is a very physical game, demanding energy, strength, and wit. The players prepare during the off-season to get ready for the preseason and eventually the season. They put their bodies through torture: pushing, pulling, pumping, jogging, running, bouncing, and all. When the actual game begins, the body and mind are already prepared for the worst. Hence, no amount of tackling or pushing or shoving intimidates the players.

The same goes for each and every one of us. The onus is on us to determine to put a foot forward. No one else will do it for us: not our parents, not our friends, not our neighbors, not the community. Our joy is only cut short when we realize that we are not ready to perform whatever task is set before us.

While it is important to improve and maintain a high professional standard, it is also of vital importance that you take good care of yourself. Don't let your responsibilities overwhelm you. That turns to stress. You need to find time to nurture the personal side of you. Get rest. Make time for personal interests. Take a walk, jog, Rollerblade, or dance. Treat yourself to a good meal. Take a vacation. Watch a good movie.

Do those little things that make you happy. It is when you are happy that your enthusiasm to accomplish unveils.

Enthusiasm

Enthusiasm is contagious. Create a sense of excitement always. Add humor to your life. Anything you find yourself doing, do it with all your heart, with gladness and appreciation of the opportunity.

I enjoyed working at Taco Bell. It was my first job in America. I washed dishes, swept the parking lot, fried tacos, cleaned the lobby, mopped the floors, and hauled the trash. I did that while attending school full-time. I know many others who share similar stories. In whichever area I found myself working on any particular day, I gave it my best with smiles and youthful exuberance.

I recall working during lunch hour one day, not knowing that the regional manager was one of the customers. He called me to the lobby and told me how impressed he was with my enthusiasm and speed. I told him I was the fastest taco maker in the world. Although I said it jokingly, he took me up on it. He challenged me to a taco-making contest with him right there. Not only did I whip out those tacos with lightning speed, but when he put the tacos on the scale, every single one of them weighed precisely three ounces. He was fast also, but I beat him. I got promoted to shift manager, the position I held until I left the restaurant after my graduation from college.

There's a story about a subway station shoe shiner who amazed people with his jokes, laughter, and enthusiasm. As he shined people's shoes, he would tell jokes. He'd throw his towel behind his back, catch it with one hand, and continue shining shoes. People would gather around to watch him shine shoes, but more importantly to be entertained by him. He caught the attention of a movie producer one day as he was doing his thing. The man gave him a business card and invited him to a meeting at the man's office. Something happened—he landed a role in a comedy movie. His life changed. He was a shoe shiner, remember. He wasn't making much money, but he enjoyed the opportunity to have something to do and the hands and energy to do it.

You are where you are for a reason. When people around you notice that you love what you do, they will want to learn from you. Recognize your ability and strength, and give yourself the opportunity to apply those strengths. Build on your interest. Celebrate successes big or small. Celebrate cultures far and near.

Your motivation must come from your passion for what you do. It must derive from your drive to accomplish a goal. In fact, you are more creative when you are enthusiastic about what you do, when you are motivated intrinsically, when you are passionate, and when you strive to achieve a goal solely for inner satisfaction. Satisfaction may come from your determination to achieve, from accepting the challenge, or from the enjoyment you derive from the work. Whatever the case may be, you must find a reason to do what you are doing. It must be a reason beyond the paycheck. Whatever your reason is, it must come from within. Dig deep for momentum, and you will not lose steam.

The satisfaction that comes with knowing that you have done the best you can is priceless. It is this satisfaction that elicits enthusiasm even in the face of difficulty. When football players advance to the field to face their opponents, they run in with enthusiasm and excitement. They are not enthusiastic because they want to intimidate their opponents. They are not excited because they are unaware of the battle ahead of them. The enthusiasm comes because the players believe that they have done all they can do. They have come with determination. They know they will be tackled, knocked down, bruised. They know there's a chance that they may have their legs or necks broken. But they have accepted the challenge ahead of time because they have made themselves ready to perform.

Enthusiasm to perform can only come when we are doing what we love to do. Why would you want to be a doctor if thinking about that kind of work depresses you? Why would you want to be a teacher if you know that you do not want to be around children? Discover your passion. Stir up the gift. Put a foot forward. Unleash your potential.

Your personal energy rejuvenates your strength as a person. Always find time to do something positive for yourself.

Now then, you are determined. You have accepted the challenge. You are ready to perform. You are enthusiastic, motivated, and encouraged. So unleash your potential! Put a foot forward—any foot!

3

You Must Stand to Unleash

Any child, to take his first step, must first of all stand. It's a natural phenomenon. Parents worry if a child passes the age of walking but has failed to stand.

In other words, standing must precede stepping. Understand also that standing does not immediately necessitate taking a first step. It gives some hope that the child will eventually step.

Notice also that when a child takes that first step, he begins to gain more confidence. However, in between the first step and the next, there is a fall. It is up to the child to stand again and try again. With time, one step at a time, he begins to walk.

What if that child refuses to stand after the first, second, and third falls? What if fear cripples him and drives away every attempt to even try again? Then a problem arises.

When Jesus met the cripple by the sea of Bethesda, He didn't just command him to arise; He also commanded him to walk (John 5:1–18). Ordinarily, when one who has been crippled stands up, the urge will be there to take that step, but perhaps the knees will not flex or the muscles will not stretch. Jesus didn't take that for granted. He knew the crippled man's fears, trepidations, anxiety, and inexperience. So Jesus gave that extra push: "Walk!"

To stand is the beginning, but you must consciously initiate a step. And taking that step doesn't guarantee a smooth walk. There will be some bumps and slips along the way, but you must persist.

You begin a new assignment or adventure, and you know it is on God's invitation. Then something begins to go wrong. The critics jump out. Imagine what the eleven in the boat were saying to Peter when he was making his plans to take the step onto the water. "He thinks he's all that. Watch and see what the wind does to him." When Peter began to sink, imagine the laughter and ridicule. But guess what? God always accomplishes His work. What He started, He will complete.

The story of the man by the pool of Bethesda is a story of missed opportunity. For many years, thirty-eight to be exact, he sat by the sea, hoping that one day he would have the opportunity to jump into the water and make his life better. Day after day, he sat and waited. Then the opportunity came: the angel of the Lord showed up and stirred the water, and whoever jumped in got healed. Many people jumped in, and their lives were never the same again. But this man, who had been crippled for many years, just could not get into the water. He was held down by a debilitating disease that had mutilated him. He was bound and held hostage by this unwanted guest.

When Jesus showed up, the man realized that he had been putting all his eggs in one basket. There is always another way. Jumping into the pool of Bethesda was a good opportunity, one the man may have missed. But there was still a better one, one that could only be brought about by the Author of life—Jesus Christ the Messiah.

Many times, we see opportunities to make our lives better, to possess our possessions, to jump into our river of blessing, and we are not able to take advantage of them when others are. By the time we decide to get in, it is too late. The best has been taken. You are sitting at the brink of success, but you can't get it.

There may have been issues in your life that have crippled you and caused you to miss opportunities to unleash your potential, to make your life better. These issues may be family concerns, work-related circumstances, or perhaps health problems. You may have given up and just want to sit and allow the certificate of your life to expire. Perhaps there's a career you wanted to pursue, or a degree you have always wanted to earn, or a business that you have always wanted to open. Don't put your eggs in one basket, as my father always told me.

The lame man put all his hope in one place—in the pool where the angel of the Lord stirred up the waters. What he didn't realize was that when one door closes, another, better door swings open. He was depressed and frustrated because he couldn't jump in the water and had no one to help him. Jesus showed up and presented a better way.

When you put a foot forward and meet what appears to be a dead end, or get knocked down by the pressures of this world, don't give up. Don't be discouraged. There is always another way, perhaps a better way, but you must first stand. You must first arise. You will never realize what you are able to do until you unleash. You will never know how far you can go until you put a foot forward—any foot!

You may be beaten down, but you can't stay beaten down. First, you have to arise. You have to take up your bed, and you have to put a foot forward. He who has called you will perfect the rest. The woman with the issue of blood heard that Jesus of Nazareth was coming to town. She was frail and weak, but she realized that she must arise and take a step of faith. Imagine her struggling through the crowd as she pushed her way to Jesus. Imagine how many times she might have fallen, yet she arose and pressed on.

Arising does not negate failure. When you arise, you will find yourself having to push through the crowd. You may be pushed down by powers stronger than you. You may face the storm of life that will toss you here and there and beat you up to hopelessness. But you must arise, and you must put a foot forward, and you must walk again.

When Peter saw Jesus walking on water, he didn't know it was Jesus, but once he confirmed His identity, Peter asked Jesus to invite him to come (Matthew 14:22–36). Peter was already standing, so when Jesus gave the invitation, there was no hesitation on Peter's part. He put a foot out of the boat, unleashed his potential, and walked on water. It was a feat no human being before him had accomplished, and one that no human being after him will ever accomplish.

Peter stood up. Then he took the step. He braved the storms of life. He knew they were boisterous, but he ignored them—momentarily.

That Peter put a foot forward did not prevent failure. Once he noticed the presence of the storm again, he began to sink. The One who had invited him to come would not let him stay sunk in the deep.

"Don't be afraid," Jesus might have whispered. "I am your God. I will strengthen you and help you. I will hold you up with my victorious right hand."

Notice that Peter was the only one in the boat who stood up. The rest were holding on for dear life, crouched in the boat. When you stand up, you elevate yourself above your present fears, worries, anxiety, and doubt; you see opportunities that would have eluded you. When you stand, your perspective widens. When you stand, you are poised to take the step.

Jesus knew that the lame man would not go anywhere unless he stood up. Jesus could have commanded him to walk, but He chose to follow the natural process and to call to our attention that walking becomes easier when we are standing. "Now that you are standing," He told the lame man, just as He is telling you and me right now, "then walk!"

A second chance

Perhaps you have had opportunities in the past that you let go by. Perhaps you have had experiences of unsuccessful ventures. There is a second chance. The Gift Giver is asking you to cast your net again the second time. Recall that Peter experienced that second-chance opportunity. He had been casting his net over and over and caught nothing. He gave up and began to clean his net. But Jesus gave him another opportunity to unleash his potential. Peter took that opportunity, and the rest is history.

The inventors of WD-40, the rust-preventive lubricant, worked on the formula over and over and failed each time. On the fortieth try, they prevailed, and that's how the number forty came to be part of the product's name. I still use WD-40 today to prevent or remove rust, and I know others do too. What if those guys had given up on the thirty-ninth attempt? I am not talking about just the first attempt. I am talking about the thirty-ninth attempt. That is persistence.

A friend and his wife applied for a home health agency license. They had admitted the required number of patients and had cared for those patients with their own money. Their resources were almost depleted. The state surveyors came after one year of waiting. My friends failed the survey. They reapplied, believing that they had learned from their mistakes. They continued to care for their patients and waited for another survey. The surveyors came again, and my friends were denied a second time. They reapplied and waited.

Relatives and friends told them to give it up and look for something else to do. Perhaps it was not what God wanted them to do. But they had spent too much money to back down now. So they cast their net again in the same waters.

Six months later, the surveyors returned, and this time my friends received their license. They are still in the business, and the rest is history.

You may have failed over and over in your attempts. You may have given up and thrown in the towel. But today, hear the voice of the Lord: "Cast your net into the deep [again] for a catch."

Recognize the opportunity

Oftentimes our eyes are blinded, such that we cannot see the blessings around us. We are so terrified by our circumstances that we lose focus. Prophet Elisha's servant was terrified when he saw the army of their enemies wanting to capture them, but when Elisha prayed and the servant's eyes opened, he saw that what he had with him was more than what was out there (2 Kings 6:15–17). When we prayerfully follow God's lead, He will help us see that what we have around us is sufficient to propel us to where He intends for us to be.

A pastor friend confessed to our Bible study group one day how he had been in prayer for God to provide his daughter with a bicycle for Christmas. One of his cousins traveling out of the country asked to be dropped off at the airport. While there, the pastor helped his cousin check in. A man ahead of them wanted to travel with a brand-new bicycle, but the airline would not allow him to check it as excess luggage. "Does anybody need a bike?" the man shouted, holding it up. Apparently, he didn't have much time to do anything else with it, and no one had come with him to the airport.

Meanwhile, my pastor friend was watching. Before he recollected himself, someone else had taken the bike. He felt bad. He had prayed for a bike. God had presented a bike to him, but he had not recognized the opportunity.

Russell Conwell, first president of Temple College, gave the famous "Acres of Diamonds" speech many years ago. In this speech, he told of a man who sold his land and went away to the ends of the earth, searching for diamonds. He died in the quest. Later, the new owner of the land found diamonds right on the property the first man had sold.

Often we fail to recognize the value of what we have. Often we go out looking for something elsewhere when it is right there in our backyards.

When I graduated from high school, I left my village to go to another state, looking for an auxiliary teaching position. After spending two years trying to overcome their stranger bias, I learned that the actual need for teachers was in my village schools and not in the city. I just hadn't recognized it. I believed the grass was greener on the other side, and those on the other side believed the grass was greener on my side.

Similarly, perhaps you have graduated from high school, and you want to go to college out of state. Other students are leaving their states to come to your state university. Well, you end up going out of state: you pay out-of-state tuition and fees, and you fly or drive back and forth for spring break, Thanksgiving, Christmas, and the rest. Then you discover that you really didn't need to be out of state in the first place. Everything you went out to look for is in your home state university.

Don't get me wrong; there are times when we really need to go out of town to look for diamonds. But there are times when we just need to do a little digging in our own yards. To do so, we must first be able to recognize a diamond when we find one, even in its raw state. Don't just leave town because your friends are leaving town. They may have gotten scholarships to do so. Don't just change jobs because you find your present job boring or uninspiring. Find out what it is that you are missing.

If you have to go, do so because you have recognized the opportunities that exist. Explore your environment. Tap into the resources that are available to you. Be creative!

Circumstances may warrant you going out of state. You may have been awarded a scholarship. That's fantastic. Then go! Sometimes your parents' situation may necessitate relocation. Then relocate! Perhaps you have been offered a better position elsewhere. Then take it!

Abraham was asked to leave his hometown to go to another place (Genesis 12:1). He obeyed, and there he found his acres of diamonds. Joseph was forced to go to Egypt (Genesis 37:36). There he found his acres of diamonds. The lepers went on their own to the camp of their enemies, out of curiosity (2 Kings 7:8). There they discovered acres of diamonds.

Whether you are asked to go or forced to go or perhaps simply decided to go on your own, out of curiosity, let wisdom guide your decision. It is the motivation that triggers the exploit. It takes patience, diligence, and commitment, but most importantly, we must work on our abilities.

The Five Abilities

The ease with which we carry out our duties and tasks, or engage in any routine, is determined by our abilities. Our abilities reflect our giftedness, and they are portrayed in the way we implement new skills.

Coaches in any sport push their players because they know there is more in them to unleash. Coaches know each of their players and know what they are capable of; hence, they will not allow them to settle for less.

As a professor, I do not allow my students to settle for less. Because I know each of them, if a completed assignment does not represent a student's ability, I require the student to redo it. Our God, the Gift Giver, knows the end from the beginning. He knew us even when we were in our mothers' wombs, even before we were conceived (Jeremiah 1:5). So He gives us the gifts according to our several abilities (Matthew 25:15). He knows our abilities, and He expects us to unleash them. As our fingerprints are different, as the inscriptions on our palms are different, so are our unique abilities.

Cap-ability

You will not know what you are capable of doing until you put a foot forward, until you unleash. God has given each one of us the capability to put our talents to good use, to unleash our potential. Do you remember Joel Osteen, the pastor of Lakewood Church in Houston? He wouldn't have known that he had the capability to become such a powerful inspiration to millions of people around the world if he hadn't put his foot forward.

You may not be a five-talent person, and you don't need to be. The capability that God has given you is to do that which He has created and called you to do. The problem, most of the time, is that we find ourselves missing the opportunities given to us to make a difference in our lives and in the lives of others.

God gave Saul the capability to succeed as the first king of Israel. Saul was handpicked; he was head and shoulders above the rest of the people. The Spirit of God was upon him, but he dropped the ball. Pain and agony followed. Before his eyes, another king was anointed.

If we fail to use the abilities that God has given us, if we fail to unleash our potential, then the Gift Giver will take what we have and give it to another.

Using our gifts does not mean that we are above mistakes. No one is. We must learn from our mistakes and try not to repeat them. We must work to improve on the things we have done and find ways to make our lives and the lives of others better.

Why did Saul fail? He was capable, but he wasn't reliable, and that cost him the throne.

Avail-ability

Availability requires sacrifice. You must be willing to give up some personal pleasures in order to achieve an expected goal. Jesus said to his disciples, "If any man will come after me, let him deny himself, and take up his cross, and follow me" (Matthew 16:24). Do not overload your schedule for yourself. Work also to make others around you better.

Availability positions you for greater opportunities. When Jesus came to the house of Mary and Martha, Martha was distracted by personal concerns. Mary, on the other hand, made herself available, and she got something "which shall not be taken away from her" (Luke 10:42).

Isaiah heard the voice of the Lord, saying, "Whom shall I send, and who will go for us?" Then he said, "Here am I; send me" (Isaiah 6:8). Once Isaiah declared his availability, God gave him a job to do for Him.

Reli-ability

Jesus spoke in a parable about a man who had two servants (Matthew 21:28–30). He asked one of the servants to go work in the vineyard. The servant said he didn't want to go, but he later changed his mind and did the work. Meanwhile, the master asked the second servant to go and do the work. The servant immediately agreed to go, but he didn't go. This servant was unreliable.

Everyone is capable, but not everyone is reliable. It is reliability that nurtures capability.

Let's say I have a good voice. I sing in the choir. The music minister appoints me to lead praise and worship on Sunday morning. But I don't show up. On Sunday morning, everything is in disarray. No one knows where I am. No one knows if I am coming or not. I haven't contacted anybody.

I come in leisurely the next Wednesday for practice. I give excuses. Too late: I may not have the chance to lead again, no matter how good my voice is, no matter how talented I am.

This is just one example. Many of us have lost such opportunities due to unreliability. We are capable but not reliable.

I used to work as a shift manager at a Taco Bell restaurant. There was an employee who was always available to work, and he always showed up on time for the lunch rush. I noticed over and over that each time I asked for replenishment of a product in the heat of the rush, such as lettuce, sour cream, cheese, black olives, or ground beef, his response was always, "Coming right at you!"

Yet then he would be at the back washing dishes, cleaning the floors, shredding lettuce. When the item that I had asked for ran out, the replacement was not there. He was capable, available, but he was not reliable. I could have fired him, but I made a decision to not schedule him again during lunch rush.

Depend-ability

Peter assured Jesus in Luke 22:33–34 that he would go with Him even unto death. But when the time came for him to make good on his promise, Peter bailed out. Jesus could not depend on him to deliver. Of course, Jesus knew that Peter was not dependable. He knew Peter would deny Him when He needed Peter most. There is nothing as good as knowing that a person will do what he says he will do.

When we are assigned to do something, we must be conscientious in getting it done to the best of our ability. Each part of the body has its function, and other parts of the body rely on each individual part to perform. The hand cannot do the work of the leg under normal circumstances; neither would the nose do the job of the eyes. People count on us to be dependable, to play our parts well and when needed. Each one of us is capable of doing what we have been created to do. The question is whether we are reliable, available, and dependable.

Account-ability

Most of the time, we try to play the blame game. Adam said it was Eve; Eve said it was the snake (Genesis 3). The bottom line is that someone messed up. The third servant buried his talent and turned around blaming his master, accusing him of reaping where he had not sown. How did the servant come up with that? It is simple; when we fail to do our part, we come up with excuses.

"I did not get the job because of my accent."

"I did not pass the exam because my professor was mean."

These are excuses. I want to hear the truth.

"I did not pass the exam because I did not prepare."

"I did not get the job because I was not qualified."

Dr. Darlington I. I. Ndubuike (Dr. D.)

The bottom line is that the Master is coming back, and He will require each one of us to give account of our talents. Will we be good and faithful servants who will find rest, or will we be the wicked servant who is doomed?

In order to unleash your potential, you must be reliable, available, and dependable. And because you are capable, you must be accountable.

4

You Must Take Off Your Shoes to Unleash

Moses's road to becoming the leader of the people of Israel was rough and winding, with several detours, but it all started because Moses put a foot forward. He saw the burning bush, and he turned aside to see (Exodus 3:3–4). It was then that he heard the voice. Perhaps if he hadn't first turned aside to see, he may not have heard the voice. He went to Egypt and unleashed his potential, but first he had to take off his shoes (Exodus 3:5). He had to shake off the dust of the past from the shoes of the present so that it did not soil the future.

Some people today literally take off their shoes before they go into a worship place. When I was growing up, I attended a church that mandated we leave our shoes outside before entering the sanctuary. So on Sundays, you would find countless shoes littered at the entryway: shoes of all makes and models, shoes of different sizes and shapes.

But the shoes we ought to have taken off were the shoes of disobedience, envy, gossip, fear, unforgiveness, anger, and more. These are the shoes of our past that will hold us back from unleashing our potential. Moses knew exactly which shoes he had on, and we do too. Those shackles must be taken off before we can freely put a foot forward and unleash our potential.

The shoe of disobedience

Disobedience can prevent us from unleashing our potential. Saul was handpicked to be the first king of Israel, but disobedience cost him his throne. Saul felt he knew better than his Maker. After all the effort and hard work of Moses, a single act of disobedience cost him entry into the Promised Land. Most times children believe they know better than their parents, especially in their teenage years. They refuse to heed the counsel of their parents and find out later that it has cost them a fortune.

Elisha served Elijah in obedience and received the mantle and the double portion of anointing thereof. Gehazi, on the other hand, disobeyed his master, and that cost him the mantle of Elisha (2 Kings 5:15–27). Most people have missed great opportunities due to disobedience. For example, many have not gotten a promotion because they were not subject to authority. Obedience goes with humility, without which you will not eat of the fruit of the land.

The shoe of envy

Envy can deprive you of your own blessing. We fail to utilize the gift we have been given because we desire someone else's gift to the extent that we begin to covet it. We fail to give thanks for what we have because we simply don't see it.

Saul sought to destroy David because he saw the gift in David. In his pursuit of David, Saul lost his peace. We desire what we don't have more than what we do have, and we end up burying our own unique gift.

That someone else is a five-talent kind of person does not mean that my one talent is not valuable. When I begin to put my one talent to good use, chances are that other doors will open for me—doors that wouldn't have opened had I failed to put a foot forward.

The shoe of gossip

Gossip is a ruthless killer. You simply destroy someone else by bearing tales that are false, or perhaps even true. But what shall it profit you to tear your brother down? We tend to forget that we sell ourselves short by doing so. Who in their right minds would want to keep you around when they know your tongue flaps uncontrollably, like an old shoelace? Gossip may even cost you a good opportunity for advancement, a good relationship, or even a good marriage.

The shoe of fear

Fear is a crippling disease. The third servant in the story of the talents had a bigger problem than he was willing to admit—fear. In Matthew 25:25, he said to his master, "And I was afraid, and went and hid thy talent in the earth".

Fear is a debilitating disease. It grinds us down to nothingness. It distorts our thought processes, and we feel incapable of putting a foot forward. We lose our sense of self. It is fear that causes us to hide our talents and prevents us from unleashing our potential.

Notice that the third servant refused to take ownership of the talent given to him. He referred to it as *"thy talent."* When the gift is given to us, it is ours. When it is given to you, it is yours. The servant didn't want to claim ownership due to fear and a sense of insecurity. He didn't believe he had the ability to do anything with his gift. Fear sank him.

We are afraid of what will happen if we fail or what people will say about us. Fear freezes us to stony rigidity that we find difficult to thaw out. But you must believe in yourself. You must understand who you are in Christ Jesus. He has not given you the spirit of fear, but of boldness, of love, and of sound mind. So I dare you to unleash your potential. I dare you to put a foot forward—any foot!

I watched as a reality show star, Kendra Wilkinson, bailed out of the show *Splash*. She had signed up. She had practiced the dives and jumps. She had the gift. But when the testing time came, she bailed out in front of millions of people. No amount of encouraging words persuaded her to change her mind. She simply gave up! She was intimidated and crippled by fear of heights. She acknowledged that she would regret that moment for the rest of her life.

Fear causes us to bail out at the edge of success. We are afraid of what will happen if we fail or what people will say about us.

The shoe of unforgiveness

Unforgiveness is a torture. Someone once described it as poison: you drink it and expect someone else to die. Imagine that you have come to present your gift to the King of kings, and He refuses to accept your gift because you are harboring unforgiveness against someone. It could be your father who left you while you were a baby, or your mother who gave you up for adoption. It could be a family member who molested you while you were young, or a friend who betrayed you. It could be your spouse who was not faithful to you or your child who disobeyed you. But if you want to unleash your potential, you have to learn to forgive.

The shoe of anger

There is nothing wrong with getting angry once in a while. After all, we are all human beings. But everything is wrong with staying angry and keeping malice. A prolonged anger can turn to wrath. Anger, if not controlled, can cause people to lose their sanity, and the outcome could be detrimental.

There's a story about a man named Mazi Dike Otinkpu, who killed himself for shame. On Orie market day, Mazi Otinkpu went to his farm to dig up some yams to sell. On his way back from the farm, Mazi Otinkpu decided to wash himself in a village river. He took off his clothes and placed them under a tree by the river.

Moments later, Eleke, the lunatic, came by and saw Mazi Otinkpu in the river bathing. He looked under the tree and saw Mazi Otinkpu's clothes. He looked at Mazi Otinkpu naked in the river, and he looked at himself, also naked. He smiled. He bent down, took the clothes, and began to put them on.

Mazi Otinkpu saw him and barked at him to put down the clothes. Eleke ignored him and continued to put on the clothes.

Mazi Otinkpu became furious. As he was getting out of the river, Eleke took off running. Mazi Otinkpu ran after Eleke, cursing and yelling with rage, "Take off those clothes right now, you crazy lunatic, before I shave your head off in one slice!"

Eleke continued to run. Mazi Otinkpu continued in pursuit. Boiling with fury and foaming with wrath, Mazi Otinkpu lost all consciousness. He fell down, got up, and continued in the chase. He totally forgot that he was naked.

Before he knew it, Eleke had run into Orie market. Mazi Otinkpu dashed into the marketplace, yelling at what now seemed to be nobody. Eleke had disappeared in the crowd. Mazi Otinkpu stood alone in the marketplace, naked, foaming with anger, dripping with sweat and dirt.

The next morning, Mazi Otinkpu's fifth wife found him hanging from a huge bamboo stem placed between two *ogirisi* trees in his yam barn. Such a death was an abomination. No one would touch him. Silence descended on the village.

5

You Must PUSH to Unleash

Prepare yourself

No soldier goes to battle unprepared. Every battlefield has its challenges, including the battlefield of life.

Let me momentarily revisit the Tyson-Douglas fight. I watched on television as Iron Mike Tyson battled Buster Douglas for the heavyweight title on February 11, 1990, in Tokyo, Japan. Mike was an undefeated champion before going into this fight. He seemed very confident that he would knock Buster Douglas out, as he had others before him. Tyson had once boasted that no man born of woman could defeat him.

What Tyson didn't know was that Douglas had prepared himself for this fight mentally and physically. Douglas came into that ring with determination and unprecedented courage. He knew he might be knocked down at some point, but he was prepared to absorb the punches and determined not to stay down.

Tyson didn't lose because he was not strong or lacked skill; he lost because he did not prepare himself. He took his opponent for granted. Even his corner came to the ring ill-prepared. Maybe they assumed that the fight would end in the first round. They didn't bring the usual medication that would be used to reduce swelling. Instead, they came with a rubber glove filled with ice, and that did not help Iron Mike's swollen eyes. Lack of preparation blinded him and cost him his destiny.

In the London Olympics, gold medal gymnast Gabby Douglas stole the hearts of everyone with her precise agility and catlike elasticity. She didn't just get up on the morning of the Olympics and decide to compete. She was sixteen years old at the time, but she had set her eyes on the gold long before the actual competition. She began the preparation in her childhood, and she knew what was involved: the physical, mental, and emotional exertion; the many hours of hard work; the strenuous exercises; the twisting and turning; the bruises; the pain. She must have fallen off the beam countless times. She must have stepped out of the line while tumbling. Her coach must have yelled at her. But she knew it was all part of the preparation to become a champion.

Before He began his ministry, Jesus spent several years preparing. He was obedient to his parents. He helped His earthly father work as a carpenter. He stayed back in the synagogue, speaking with the elders and doctors, at age twelve. We don't hear about him again until He is thirty years old. He spent eighteen years preparing to unleash His potential.

Then He spent forty days in the wilderness, fasting and praying. Then He was baptized by John the Baptist. Then He faced grueling temptation by the devil.

Jesus likewise prepared His disciples for ministry. He taught them over and over in many ways, through parables, beatitudes, and miracles. He spent time preparing them for His departure and the great commission. He ate a last supper with them at the upper room. That preparation gave the disciples the boldness to unleash their potential.

When Peter and John came to the gate called Beautiful, Peter didn't hesitate to put his foot forward. He had been prepared for this. He had been with Jesus, and he knew he got it. He unleashed his potential, and then something happened—the lame man rose up and walked!

Great things happen when we are prepared. Students cannot watch television all day and expect to make good grades. Frustration sets in when we are ill-prepared. You can't go to college and expect to major in medicine when you lack high school preparation in the sciences. You can't expect to succeed as an engineering major if you lack high school math skills.

Gabby Douglas knew what she wanted to become, and she began preparing for it right from childhood. We are often afraid to put a foot forward and unleash our potential simply because we have not prepared ourselves.

Understand who you are

When the angel of the Lord appeared to Gideon, the angel addressed him as "the mighty man of valor" (Judges 6:12). Gideon began a series of arguments that revealed his lack of understanding of who he was. In fact, he placed himself at such a low level that only an angel of the Lord could bring him up. His mental image of himself was so low that he thought he was not capable of accomplishing anything. He even asked for signs to cure his self-doubt.

Perhaps my family is poor, my parents are divorced, and I live in a run-down neighborhood. These are some of the excuses of Gideon. Gideon had to first change his thought process and understand that he had what it took to unleash his potential and be victorious. It was his state of mind that put him in a corner.

You know yourself better than anybody else. You know your habits and what motivates you. You know your study pattern. You know the things that cause you stress. You know how you think, how you relate to others, what you like to wear, and what your body can and cannot tolerate.

You don't want to do something because someone else is doing it. You know what pleases you and displeases you. You don't want to jump because someone else is jumping. Your body must say "jump" before you take that leap. Knowing who you really are will determine what you can really do.

Everyone is uniquely gifted. When you discover your unique gift, don't hesitate to put a foot forward. I have always believed that I can do all things through Christ who strengthens me. This is not just a saying; it is the word of God.

Unless you understand yourself, you will have difficulty putting a foot forward. It is your knowledge of yourself, your abilities, your emotions, and your physicality that must drive your effort to unleash.

In the city where I live, there is a skilled, popular furniture seller, "Mattress Mark," who is very enthusiastic about his trade. He takes pride in the quality of furniture he sells to society. He works with the furniture that comes ready to assemble with the same passion and attention that he works with the furniture that comes broken or with pieces missing. He does not return broken pieces of furniture. He repairs it and creates matching pieces such that the finished work has no mark of brokenness. He knocks on his furniture to demonstrate its solidity and readiness. He guarantees comfort and immediate delivery with no back orders.

What implication does this have for you? You must cultivate the attitude of that furniture seller. You must show that you love what you do and commit to "immediate delivery without back-order slips." Your job is to fashion the most beautiful piece of fine furniture from the wood you have. It doesn't matter what forest the wood came from; it doesn't matter what color, shape, or form the wood has. Your task is the same—to make beautiful furniture suitable for the market.

It doesn't matter if you are a raw log. It doesn't matter if you are half-broken or have missing parts. It doesn't matter if you are already processed and ready to assemble. Your family may have despised you. You may have lived on food stamps or been raised in a homeless shelter. The onus is still on you to fashion yourself into fine furniture suitable for market.

You must believe that you are capable of succeeding and moving on to higher levels, regardless of ability or background. We must fix the "broken" parts of us. We must find suitable matches for the "missing" parts. It is our responsibility to make ourselves suitable for the marketplace.

Whether the wood makes it to the market depends on your ability and skill as a furniture seller, your patience and courage, your persistence and tenacity, and most importantly, your understanding of the direction of your grain. The grain represents who you are and what drives you, your interests and lived experiences.

In other words, you must look into your BACKPACK—your background, ability, cultural orientation, knowledge, personality, attitude, communication pattern, and keep.

It is the failure to chisel with the grain that causes wood to chip. What is your grain? Do you carve with it or against it?

Sacrifice

When Elijah went to the widow of Zarephath, a very interesting set of events took place (1 Kings 17:8–16). Elijah was hungry, and he came to a poor widow. He asked for water. That was easy. The widow didn't hesitate to give him water to drink.

Then Elijah asked for food. All the widow had was a little flour and oil. She immediately made Elijah understand that she was going to prepare that for herself and her son to eat. Then they would die.

Elijah insisted that she allow him to eat first, and promised her that she would never run out of oil and flour if she did. Even though this was the widow's last meal, she was willing to give it up in faith. She put a foot forward. It might not have been her best foot. What mattered was that she unleashed her potential. She literally gave all that she had. Then something happened—and her life was never the same.

Sacrifice does not necessarily involve money or food. It can be a habit that negatively impacts your ability to take that step. It can be past experiences, guilt, or hurt. You must give it all up.

Sacrifice is also about giving up certain pleasures of the moment in order to attain a goal, to reach a destiny. It is about giving of yourself. When Jesus told the disciples that curing the boy possessed by an evil spirit could only be done by fasting and prayer, it implied sacrifice. Blood was shed for our redemption. This is an ultimate sacrifice.

When Elijah called Elisha according to the will of God in 1 Kings 19:15–21, Elisha knew the calling was of God, and he quickly heeded it. What happened next? Elisha gave up all he had—his oxen, his farm, and his family—and followed Elijah. Guess what else happened? In 2 Kings, Elisha's fame as the prophet of the living God is said to have spread like wildfire all through Israel and beyond. God used him mightily to perform great signs and wonders in the land.

Following Moses's burning bush experience, God told him to yield his staff, to let go. Now, Moses had had that staff for a long time. In fact, it was almost his life companion through those rough experiences in the desert. God told him to drop it.

So Moses obeyed. He let go of his staff. Then God asked him to pick it up again. When Moses picked up the same staff he had surrendered, it was no longer the staff of Moses. It had transformed into the staff of God. Moses did not go to Egypt with his staff; he went to Egypt with the staff of God.

It is incredible that when we obey God and give up that which we think belonged to us, God assumes responsibility for us and causes us to do the impossible.

Again, when God told Moses to take off his sandals, Moses obeyed. He took them off. When he put them back on, God had stretched the life span of those sandals. Moses didn't have to change sandals all through the time God used him to lead the children of Israel out of Egypt.

When Jesus told Peter to cast his net again for a catch, Peter's argument was that of an experienced professional in his field of endeavor. He had been a fisherman all his life, and he apparently knew when there was something left in the waters. But when he decided to yield his knowledge, experience, and expertise to the command of Jesus, he cast his net again (Luke 5:1–10). The net that once belonged to Peter, an expert fisherman, instantly transformed into the net of Jesus, the Master Fisher of Men. From nothing, Peter caught a shoal.

Sometimes we think we know it all and no one can tell us anything. We allow the opportunity of a lifetime to elude us due to arrogant ignorance. To put a foot forward and unleash our potential, we must be willing to let go, to yield, to surrender, and to sacrifice.

Can you imagine surrendering your business and its finances at the command of God today, totally, and watching it transform into the business and finances of God? Can you imagine surrendering your life to God today and watching your life transform into the image of Christ, instantly?

When God told Abraham to leave his hometown, where he had been raised and had stayed all his life, God was asking him to make a sacrifice, to give it up. Abraham obeyed, and he reaped the benefit of his obedience.

This was the experience the rich young ruler missed. Jesus asked him to surrender his wealth, but he held on tightly and missed the transforming opportunity of a lifetime. Perhaps he someday read about the experiences of Elisha and Moses and the widow and how their lives had changed, and wished he had given up his wealth for wealthier rewards. But by then it was too late. He had missed the opportunity of a lifetime.

Perhaps God opened a door for you to attend college in another state far away from home, but you wanted to go to the same college where your friends were. You refused the offer to relocate, and you missed the opportunity of a lifetime. Or perhaps God wanted you to stay at a local university, but your friends were moving out of town to attend college, and you didn't want to stay around your parents. You relocated on your own, and then you discovered that you had missed the opportunity of a lifetime.

A lady came to me one day after church service and asked me to pray for her. She had retired, and she wanted to do something to make her life better. She had chosen to go into the home health business at a time when the market was tight and a lot of money was required to establish such a business. She was confident that she was going to make it. According to her, she had put all her retirement money into the business, and she was determined to make it work.

We held hands and prayed. What struck me was more than her determination and acceptance of the challenges; it was her sacrifice. She simply put all she had into this, believing that the Master of the Gifts would reward her effort with success. All she did was put a foot forward. It might not have been her best foot, but it was her foot!

"The best is yet to come," my father would always tell me. Perhaps I have a major exam on Monday, but my best friend has a birthday party on Sunday night. The party organizers have promised a night full of food, drinks, and merrymaking. I must know how to make a decision not to attend that party, because there is something better ahead of me. The party will be held again next year, but if I flunk that major exam, I am sunk.

When my son was in elementary school, he loved to watch *The Cosby Show*. Every day after school, he would flip the channel for *The Cosby*

Show. One day, I called him to his room and told him that *The Cosby Show* would always be there, and even better shows would come later, but the opportunity to complete his homework would not wait for him. If he failed to study, he would not graduate, and yet the shows would continue to run. He heeded.

I love football. Say that I have been given a free ticket to attend a game. But I have a major presentation at the office the following day, a life-changing presentation. I must decide to give the ticket to somebody else and concentrate on that presentation. I must sacrifice the pleasure of the moment for a better life ahead. I must make a decision to put that foot forward.

This might not be a great example of the kind of sacrifice intended, but it gives you an idea: you have to give in order to get something better, and sometimes you have to give something you enjoy a lot.

Humble yourself

When Jesus came to where Peter and his friends were fishing, He asked Peter to cast his net into the deep for a catch (Luke 5:1–10). Remember that Peter was a professional fisherman. Arrogance would have said, "Wait a minute, Jack! I know these waters. I have been fishing all my adult life in these waters. I know when there are fish to catch and when to draw up the nets."

But in his humility, Peter recognized that no one knows it all. He acceded to a second chance. "Master, at your word, I will cast the net again!" When Peter let go of all that pride, arrogance, and boastfulness, and humbled himself, something happened—his life changed forever.

When I came to America, the land of my dreams, I didn't quite find what I thought I would find. I had university degrees before I came here. I had taught in elementary and secondary schools in my home country. I thought I was going to have a smooth transition.

The first place I went to look for a job was at a school district. Then I went to a museum, and then to a theater downtown. Yeah, right! You know, I thought I was all that *and a bag of chips*! I found out the hard way.

I ended up working at Taco Bell, cleaning the parking lot, washing dishes, frying tacos, shredding lettuce, and all the other tasks that come up in a fast-food restaurant.

The voice of arrogance said, "I'm not gonna do this! Do you know me? Do you want to see my credentials? I was a teacher back home in my country."

Then humility countered, "Boy, please! Keep that to yourself. This is America, Jack!"

So I managed to put all that bragging behind, put on my uniform, and get dirty. I had to do it in order to have the opportunity to unleash my potential.

Naaman, the great Syrian general, had a test of humility as well. He didn't want to wash in the river Jordan, as Elisha the prophet commanded (2 Kings 5). Listen to the voice of arrogance once again: "Who does he think he is? Does he know who I am? I am a Syrian army general, for crying out loud! I have better rivers in my home country."

Then humility countered, "Boy, please! Keep that to yourself. This is Israel, Jack!"

Naaman put a foot forward. It wasn't his best foot. It was a foot of humility, humility he didn't have in the first place but had to find in order to unleash his potential. Then something remarkable happened— he had a better life after.

You see, humility does not stem from our position in life. Neither does arrogance, nor pride. Attitude and disposition govern our behavior.

Naaman was not prideful and arrogant simply because he was a Syrian army general. After all, he was a leper. He should have been an outcast, for crying out loud. What blinded him was ignorance.

The centurion who met Jesus in Matthew 8:5–10 was also an army general. His servant was sick, and he came looking for the great Physician. He didn't send his servants to fetch Jesus. When Jesus told him He would come to his house, his response was chilling: "Lord, I do not deserve to have you come under my roof but just say the word and my servant will be healed" (Matthew 8:8). His humility got the attention of Jesus, and He said He had not found such faith in Israel.

In the context of this discussion, I would say I have not found such humility in the world: the humility of the King of kings who willingly offered to go to the house of the centurion, and the centurion who declared himself unworthy of such royal visitation!

Now, the centurion's act may not sound like what you would do. Perhaps you would do something else. But whoever wants to unleash his potential must put a foot forward. Our best foot might be arrogance or pride, but we need a foot of humility. "If my people, which are called by my name, shall humble themselves, and pray, and seek my face, and turn from their wicked ways; then I will hear from heaven, and I will forgive their sin, and will heal their land" (2 Chronicles 7:14). What a promise!

6

You Must STEP to Unleash

When Peter took that bold step outside the boat, he wasn't thinking about being the first human to ever walk on water. He just saw the opportunity of a lifetime, an invitation to unleash his potential. We aren't told which foot Peter put out first. The important thing was that he took the step.

That step was not an ordinary step. It was a life-changing STEP. Peter *seized* the opportunity, *took* action by faith, *encouraged* himself in the Lord, and *prayerfully* followed God's lead.

Taking the STEP does not guarantee an uninterrupted walk on water. You will certainly encounter some storm along the way and some sinking sensation. Then your critics will have a field day.

Imagine what Peter must have heard from the rest of the disciples still in the boat, shivering with fear. They were too afraid to unleash, and they wanted to discourage someone who had the boldness to brave the wind. Imagine what they said when they saw Peter beginning to sink.

"We told him so."

"He thought he was all that."

But Peter didn't stay sunk in the deep.

Seize the opportunity

When Moses encountered the burning bush, he didn't let that spectacular sight pass him by (Exodus 3). He didn't know what it was.

He hadn't seen anything like that in his life. But he said, "I will now turn aside and see this great sight, why the bush is not burnt" (Exodus 3:3). He could have run away in fear or simply ignored it, but he seized the opportunity, realizing perhaps it could be the opportunity of a lifetime, and it was indeed.

God could have used anybody. Perhaps if Moses had missed the opportunity, someone else would have seized it. It was only "when the Lord saw that he turned aside to see [that] God called unto him out of the midst of the bush" (Exodus 3:4).

Pastor Joel Osteen, as described in an earlier chapter, picked up the mantle that fell from his father. When this opportunity came, he could have declined it. He could have responded like Gideon during his initial encounter with the angel of the Lord, or like Moses during his initial encounter with God Himself. The pastor's stomach may have turned over, and his heart may have pounded a million times a second, but he was determined to seize the opportunity. It was the opportunity of a lifetime.

I was a foreign student in an American college and paid foreign student tuition. Most of my American friends had some type of scholarship or financial aid, and they frequented the financial-aid office. I didn't pay attention to it because I didn't think I could qualify for financial aid as a foreign student with no residency status.

One day, one of my friends asked me to go with him to the financial-aid office. I did. I saw a financial-aid booklet on the counter titled "Financial Aid Q&A." I picked up the booklet and looked through it while I was waiting for my friend to conclude his visit. As I thumbed the pages, I bumped into a section titled, "Who Can Qualify for Financial Aid?" I discovered that I too could get financial aid, even as a foreign student. I could qualify to receive financial aid due to good grades.

I thought, *Are you kidding me?* I read all about it, turned in my application, and received money for that semester. That encouraged me to continue to strive to keep my grades at a qualifying level, semester after semester.

This may not be a great example of seizing the opportunity. You may have a better example. The bottom line is that I picked up the bulletin even when I didn't think any good thing could come out of it for me.

God actually took me to that "burning bush," and all I did was turn aside to see. The rest is history.

The opportunity before you could be the opportunity of a lifetime, perhaps the only opportunity at all. When I was growing up, the saying was that opportunity knocks but once.

When the blind man in Luke 18:15–43 heard that Jesus of Nazareth was passing by, he seized the opportunity. He cried out in a loud voice for Jesus. Again, he took the step, and he received criticism from those around him. If he had shied away out of intimidation, he would have missed the opportunity of a lifetime.

In fact, the more they criticized, the more they discouraged, the more they tried to silence him, the louder he cried out. Then Jesus stood still. The King of kings stood still for a blind man, for a beggar, for a pauper. Why? Because the blind man seized the opportunity and took action by faith.

There was a paralytic in the city of Capernaum, and he had been in that state of health for a long time (Luke 5:17–26). When his friends heard that Jesus was coming to Capernaum, they knew it was the opportunity of a lifetime. They knew their friend could not get to Jesus by himself, and he might never have such an opportunity again. They had heard about Jesus, and they knew He had the answer to this problem.

Without hesitation, they seized the opportunity. When they brought their friend to the house where Jesus was, they faced an obstacle. There was no way to get to Jesus. The whole place was packed full with a throng of people. They did not take their friend back to his house. They did something remarkable; they took action by faith, and you know the rest of the story—their friend received healing!

My wife was pregnant with our second child while she was in nursing school. She requested to enroll in the evening program because it would be more convenient for us, since I attended school during the day. The admissions office told her that the odds were slim, but if someone else dropped out, my wife would get a chance.

My wife didn't give up. She continued to call the office for that one chance. One day when she called, they told her that someone had just dropped out. If she could come to the office right away, she could sign up for the evening program.

I was still at school, and there was no one at home. We only had one car, and none of our friends were available to take her. My wife called a cab and took our little son with her. To her, it was the opportunity of a lifetime. She seized it, and the rest is history.

My wife called the cab because she knew it was God who had opened that door. She took action by faith.

Take action by faith

When Peter put his foot forward, he didn't know exactly what was going to happen next, but he took that step anyway. The journey of life is taken one step at a time. The door will slide open as you step up to it. Some may be automatic doors; with others, you may have to do a little pushing or pulling.

Abraham was told to leave his father's house and go to a land he didn't know. He wasn't sure where he was going, but he took the step anyway. Would you be willing to leave the comfort of your environment to go teach in a remote country in response to God's call? Would you be willing to take a menial job assignment, even if you knew you were overqualified for it?

When the friends of the paralyzed man saw that there was no way to get to Jesus, they went up to the roof, tore the roof apart, and lowered their friend directly to the feet of Jesus. They didn't think about the owner of the house. How would the roof be fixed? Who would pay for it? Those issues didn't deter them. They saw the opportunity of a lifetime: Jesus was in the picture, and that was all that mattered. They seized the opportunity and took action by faith.

Moses took his family and rode on a donkey back to Egypt. He knew the imminent danger, but because he had heard from God, he put his faith into action. He unleashed, and you know the rest of the story. Moses could have shied away; he attempted to. He gave all the excuses he could think of. He might have even doubted the power of God and what He could do.

The bottom line is that Moses took the step. It wasn't easy for Moses when he unleashed, but he was not alone. He who made the opportunity available was with him all the time. Faith has to be the watchword as you take the step. You may not see everything ahead or in store, but He who called you will equip you. As the songwriter says, just "trust and obey, for there's no other way" (John H. Sammis, 1846–1919).

David perhaps didn't know what he was getting himself into when he went to the camp of the Israelites to visit. Could he have gone there by accident? I would say the answer is *no*. It was a divine intervention, a divine assignment. David could have shied away from the towering giant, Goliath. He could've listened to his brother, who didn't want him to be there. But David listened to God. David took a step of faith. He knew that God had been with him in the past against lions and bears, so he trusted this God, knowing that He would do it again.

You see, when you take a step, there will be people who will discourage you. They will try to talk you out of seizing the opportunity and taking action by faith.

We saw Peter earlier as he stepped out of the boat. Imagine what was going through his mind. Imagine what the other eleven were saying to him. He could have given up and stayed in the boat with the others, but he took that step against all the boisterous wind of taunting, discouragement, criticism, and gossip.

The frail little old lady with the issue of blood whom we saw earlier heard that Jesus was coming through. Recall that she had been sick for twelve years. She knew this was the opportunity of a lifetime. The great Physician had come to her neighborhood. She took action by faith! No one could stop her: not her friends, not her foes. She struggled through the pressing crowd. She was pushed, shoved, and knocked over, but she didn't want to miss this opportunity. She fell down, she got up, and she pressed on.

When she touched Jesus, action collided with faith to the second power. The great Physician made a public confession that power had gone out of him.

We also saw Pastor Joel Osteen earlier. He saw the opportunity of a lifetime, and he seized it. Then he took action by faith, and the rest is history. You see, it's not about how strong. It's not about how big. It's not about how swift. It's not about how smart or eloquent. It's about whosoever will. It is about recognizing the opportunity of a lifetime, seizing it, and taking action by faith.

Encourage yourself in the Lord

No one has said that the road will be easy. As a matter of fact, the responsibilities get tougher as you ascend the ladder and progress in your path. But you must encourage yourself in the Lord. It is not about what you can do, but about what God can do through you. "It is not by power; it is not by might; it is by My Spirit," says the Lord God of Hosts (Zachariah 4:6).

David understood this principle. In 1 Samuel 30, when he returned to Ziklag and found the place in ruins and all inhabitants taken away, he wept. Pain and anguish engulfed him, and he was greatly distressed. Even in his helpless state, his friends spoke of stoning him, as if it were his fault, "but David encouraged himself in the Lord" (1 Samuel 30:6).

Pastor Joel Osteen didn't think it was going to be easy when he made the determination to seize the opportunity. He knew there would be storms along the way, and there have been, but he continues to encourage himself in the Lord.

Things got tougher as my wife progressed in her pregnancy. She continually experienced exhaustion and weakness, but she had to pass all her exams to continue in the nursing program. She continued to encourage herself in the Lord. Somehow, she found strength knowing that she was not in this alone. She knew somehow that she been admitted to nursing school because it was the will of God for her. She knew that her acceptance in the evening program against all odds was a miracle. She held on.

Perhaps you have seized that opportunity and have taken that step of faith, and you have come to a point where you are beginning to wonder if you did the right thing. You are distressed and confused and full of doubt. Perhaps some of your friends are beginning to gossip and taunt. Things are rough for you and getting tougher. I say to you right now, encourage yourself in the Lord. If God is with you, who can be against you? Be still and know He is God.

When I received a letter of admission from the University of Houston several years ago, I had just completed my higher national diploma and been offered a good job. To leave my home country then would mean losing the benefit of many years of hard work. I only had enough money to relocate and rent a place in the city of my new employment. The money I had was not even enough to purchase a plane ticket to the United States.

I told the friends with whom I had graduated what had just happened. They laughed, perhaps cynically. Some advised me to work for some years first before considering going abroad. They told me that many people had gone to the United States and hurriedly returned due to hardship.

I thought about it for weeks. I knew I still had some time to decide. To make a long story short, one night as I was praying, it dawned on me that this could be the opportunity of a lifetime. My thought process changed.

Upon my arrival in the United States, I discovered that some of the things those people had said were true. Things got really tough, and there was no help coming from anywhere. But I knew within me that I hadn't made the move alone; God was in it. Like David, I encouraged myself in the Lord.

God always pursues His word to perform it. He does what He says He will do. We must encourage ourselves in the Lord, knowing that He is faithful who promised (Hebrews 10:23).

Encourage yourself with God's presence, His promise, and His power. He said, "I am with you every step [STEP] of the way." When you seize the opportunity and take that action by faith, and you find that things are beginning to go wrong, don't be discouraged. His presence is with you. His presence was with Paul and Silas in prison. His presence was with Daniel in the lions' den. His presence was with Joseph in the pit. His presence was with the three Hebrew boys in the fiery furnace. His presence was with David against Goliath.

If you find yourself jailed by circumstances or decisions you have made, rest assured that He will open the doors for you. If you find yourself thrown in the lions' den, know that He will close the mouths of the lions for your sake. If you find yourself thrown in the fire, know that He is in the fire with you, and you will not be scorched. When you find yourself in a pit, know He will send caravan your way. He will not let you be destroyed. When you are facing a giant, no matter what the giant represents, know that He is there. When Peter began to sink after taking action by faith, Jesus was there to lift him up.

God's promises are always "Yes," and we say "Amen" to them. He promised that He will never leave us nor forsake us. He didn't forsake Joshua. He didn't forsake Gideon. He didn't forsake Peter. He didn't forsake Esther. It is easy to despair, but encourage yourself in His promises.

When David discovered that he had lost everything to the enemy, he was discouraged. Even his own men abandoned him. They wanted to kill him in anger, but David remembered God's presence and promises. He secluded himself to be with his God. He didn't ask God why. He didn't cry to God for sympathy. He began to exalt the name of the Lord. He sang His praises, and in the process, his focus shifted altogether to the Lord of Hosts.

Have you come home and discovered that your house has burned down? Have you come home and discovered that your lights are turned off? Have you checked your mailbox and found that you didn't get that job? What is it that has caused you to despair? You can do as David did. Encourage yourself in the Lord. Sing praises unto Him. He is more than able to do exceedingly and abundantly above and beyond our expectations. Stand on His promises.

The Lord in the midst of you is mighty. He made the heavens and the earth with His spoken word. This is the God you serve. He is powerful. He parted the Red Sea. He healed the sick. He raised the dead. He walked upon the water. Nothing is impossible with Him. Therefore, be strong and of good courage!

Prayerfully follow God's lead

Staying close to God is paramount when you take that step. When David found out that he had lost everything, he agonized, but he didn't allow his emotions to overrule his sense of reason. Instincts would have driven him to pursue his enemies right away, but he knew that he could do nothing by himself. So David inquired of the Lord, and God gave him victory (1 Samuel 30:8). When God is leading, no one can stand in the way. In the end, David recovered everything.

When Abraham took his family and left the comfort of their hometown, he didn't know where he was going. He followed God's lead day by day. As long as we don't go ahead of God in our daily journey through life, we are guaranteed a safe arrival at our destination. God prepares us before He moves us to the next level. When God initiates it, He will bring it to completion.

Peter experienced that firsthand. Jesus initiated the invitation for Peter to come, and Peter stepped out in obedience, following Jesus's lead. Jesus didn't allow him to be drowned by the raging waters because, as He spoke through Isaiah the prophet, He planned it in the first place, and He completed it (Isaiah 46:11).

But when we go ahead of God and try to crookedly finagle our way to a position or place we have not been prepared for, the end result can be very devastating. Saul experienced that firsthand. He was the king, and he thought he could go ahead of God. He did, and he suffered the consequences (1 Samuel 15:1–35).

When the angel of the Lord appeared to Gideon, he addressed Gideon as a "mighty man of valor" (Judges 6:12). Gideon felt the weight of that title on his shoulders right away, and he panicked. "No, no, no, no, no! Please give it to someone else. I am not qualified to bear that title. I don't have the skill. My parents are poor." But when he eventually determined to accept the challenge, he took the STEP. He seized the opportunity, he took action by faith, he encouraged himself in the Lord, and he prayerfully followed God's lead. You know the rest of the story—he unleashed his potential, and the Midianites fell by the sword.

When Moses saw the burning bush, the Lord called out to him. Eventually God gave him a title, "like God to Pharaoh" (Exodus 7:1). Moses busted out, "Wha-wha-wha-what! Who am I to be God to mighty Pharaoh? Please give that assignment to someone else." But when he eventually determined to accept the challenge, he took the STEP. You know the rest of the story—he unleashed his potential, and the Israelites were freed from bondage.

When Pastor Joel Osteen realized that he was the one to lead the largest church in the world, I bet you he had plenty of excuses. "I'm not prepared to be a pastor. I can't speak in front of a huge audience. I'm not eloquent. I'm not really the next in line. Could you give that position to my big brother? What about my mom?"

I have made up those excuses, but they could have been going through his mind during that moment. Pastor Joel Osteen seized the opportunity, took action by faith, encouraged himself in the Lord, and prayerfully followed God's lead. He put a foot forward, and he unleashed his potential.

We all have excuses. Fear and doubt rob us of the opportunities of a lifetime. But God has not given us the spirit of fear. He has given us the spirit of boldness and sound mind. With such boldness, David took the STEP against the great Philistine giant. David witnessed Goliath intimidating the children of God. We saw earlier how David seized the opportunity against all odds. He took action by faith; he encouraged himself in the Lord. He knew that the same God who had been with him in the wilderness when he battled and killed lions and bears would be with him again. He prayerfully followed God's lead, and you know the rest of the story—he unleashed his potential, and the great giant fell.

You cannot know what you are capable of doing until you take that STEP. When we trust God and follow His lead, we will not go ahead of Him.

Following God's lead involves waiting, because you cannot go ahead of God. His timing is different, and you must exercise enormous patience. Peter did not hurriedly jump out of the boat when he knew the vision before him was Jesus. He prayerfully inquired of the Lord for direction. He took the step because Jesus said "Come," and he was certain he had heard the voice of Jesus.

Don't jump into situations or make hasty decisions. Don't try to outsmart God. Don't try to help Him help you. Surrender, and let Him do what He has said He will do in His own time. Abraham and Sarah lost patience in waiting, and the consequences were devastating. Saul lost patience in waiting, and as soon as he offered the sacrifice, Prophet Samuel showed up. We tend to give up on the brink of success. All we have to do is wait on the Lord and be of good courage.

Dr. Darlington I. I. Ndubuike (Dr. D.)

I graduated from high school with one of the best results achievable, known then as grade one. I was granted admission to a university to study law, but I couldn't go because my father could not afford the tuition.

It was during that period that my country's government approved a universal primary education program and gave people free training to become teachers. Instead of just sitting there, I seized the opportunity and put a foot forward. It was not my best foot, but it was my foot. I applied and was selected to attend the teacher training program.

I was the only one in my class with a grade one. Others with such high grades had gone to different universities or other institutions of higher learning. It was not an easy kernel for me to swallow, but I went through with it. After graduating from the teacher college, I taught in elementary and secondary schools in my country.

When the time came, God moved me and set my feet on higher ground. I attended a higher teacher education college, and then I moved on to the Institute of Management and Technology. I had thought I was wasting my time, going around in circles. What I didn't realize then was that I was waiting for the Lord, and that God was actually preparing me to become the teacher of the year at an American public school, and then a dean's faculty excellence award recipient as a professor at a university in America.

I appreciate the Psalmist when he said, "Wait on the Lord, be of good courage, and He shall strengthen thy heart: wait, I say, on the Lord" (Psalm 27:14). And again in Isaiah: "They that wait on the Lord shall renew their strength" (Isaiah 40:31).

Taking the STEP requires self-discipline. A few years ago, my senior pastor shared his vision with the congregation. He had been in prayer, and he asked the congregation to join him in this prayer for God to give us southwest Houston. And so it was. For many years after, the congregation prayed collectively and individually.

Then something happened. My senior pastor received a call: "Come over to our church and help us!" A church was facing great difficulty meeting its financial obligations. It was on the verge of bankruptcy, and someone had to take it over or it would be foreclosed.

Something remarkable happened—the call came to my pastor to consider taking over the affairs of the church. He had been praying for southwest Houston, and God had given him a significant part of southwest Houston.

But the senior pastor didn't jump headlong into it with reckless abandon. Without letting the congregation know, he went back to God in prayer and fasting. Then he called the other pastors and members of the deacon board and presented the proposal to them. Then the deacon board and the pastors went into prayer and fasting. While in prayer and fasting, the hearts of the deacon board, the pastors, and the senior pastor began to beat as one. They all had peace about it, and there was no question in their minds that they were hearing from God.

My senior pastor had not prayed for a church to go bankrupt. He had not prayed for a church to be foreclosed upon. His prayer and desire had always been to build the kingdom of God. He always said, "We are not here to build a church. We are not here to build a reputation for ourselves. We are here to build the kingdom of God." He encouraged members to search out those who were *unchurched*—in other words, those who didn't have a home church—and invite them to our church. He encouraged those who already had a home church to continue to be faithful where God had placed them. He didn't know by what means God would give us southwest Houston.

So, when the call for help came, the senior pastor agonized over it because it was not his desire for any church to experience such a disaster. That church property was at the mercy of the bank. The bank could sell it to anybody for any use. It could have become a club or a car lot. But God wanted to build His kingdom.

When my senior pastor confirmed the call was from God to build His kingdom, he went to the deacon board and the pastors. When the pastors and the deacon board gave their consent after fasting and prayer, my senior pastor brought the call to the congregation. An emergency business meeting was called. He presented the situation to the congregation and gave everyone an opportunity to air his or her view of the proposal. There was an open microphone, and people asked questions and made comments. The congregation prayed, and at the end of it, the congregation voted.

The vote was overwhelming in favor. Out of the entire congregation, there were fewer than fifteen "no" votes. That was an overwhelming affirmation of God's will.

My senior pastor's approach to this decision mirrored Peter's walk on water. When Peter first saw a figure walking on water, he wasn't sure who it was. Then he realized it was Jesus. Peter could have just jumped into the water at that point, since the figure was his Master. But Peter first confirmed with Jesus, "Is it you?"

Even with Jesus's response, "It is I, do not be afraid," Peter still didn't jump into the water right away.

Peter said to Jesus, "If it is you, command me to come."

Even when Jesus said "Come," Peter still didn't jump into the water. He took a STEP out of the boat, and one step after another, he began to walk on water.

When the opportunity arose for my senior pastor to reach more people in southwest Houston, he didn't just jump into it, even though he knew the call came from Jesus. He went into fasting and prayer, asking Jesus, "Is it you?"

Even when Jesus said to him, "It is I, do not be afraid," the pastor still didn't make the decision to proceed.

The pastor asked Jesus, "If it is you, command me to come."

Even when Jesus said to him "Come," he still didn't unilaterally decide to make the move. He went to the pastors and the deacon board, and finally to the congregation.

The unanimous vote of all the pastors and the deacon board, and the overwhelming approval by the congregation were significant. They recognized the opportunity, and they took the STEP. They seized the opportunity, they took action by faith, they encouraged themselves in the Lord, and they prayerfully followed God's lead.

Many people in the congregation were excited to visit our new church campus immediately, but our senior pastor sent an e-mail message with the subject line, "DON'T COME TO CHURCH!" It got everyone's attention.

He later explained what he meant. "We are not going to rush things," he told us. "We are going to follow the lead of God in this. We still have a lot of work to do." He acknowledged that there would be bumps in the road, but he reminded us that God promised He would be with us every step of the way. He will build His church and the gate of hell shall not prevail against it!

7

You Need CASH to Unleash

It has often been said that cash is king. Literally speaking, your purchasing power is determined by the amount of cash you have at your disposal. The more of it you have, the more you can purchase.

The same is true about how effectively you can unleash your potential. The more CASH you have, the better your chances of putting a foot forward. Your CASH is your charisma, attitude, skill, and honesty.

Charisma

You are a special person, and you must understand that. Holding your head up is a good place to start. You don't have to walk around feeling dejected or intimidated. You don't have to be someone else. You simply have to be you.

There has to be something about you that draws people to you. Being charismatic is being noticeable. Whenever you come into a place, people cannot help but notice that someone special has entered. Your friends and even people you do not know want to emulate you. You don't have to have plenty of money. You don't have to be tall and handsome. It is the confidence that you have in yourself, that adorable persona, that will propel you to greater heights.

When you are charismatic, you are not intimidated. Confidence allows you to put a foot forward and take that step. Once you know who you are and can identify your abilities, then you will begin to do the things you love to do. You will walk with greater confidence, unmistakable identity, irreplaceable presence, unruffled demeanor, and indefatigable stride.

Attitude

One thing that can restrain you from unleashing your potential is a negative attitude. I have heard people say that it is attitude that determines altitude.

When I was a little boy, I wanted very much to go to school. I was determined to do whatever it took to go to school. I had a burning desire to learn. This desire generated my self-confidence and determination to achieve my goal. I even worked on people's farms and hunted rabbit to raise funds for school.

I was sometimes put down, ridiculed, and rejected, but in my heart, I knew I had a gift. I didn't want anything to stop me from using it. When the time came for me to start school, I was grateful for the opportunity.

On the other hand, when a person doesn't want to do anything, perhaps because he has been ridiculed, rejected, and put down before, it affects his thinking. He will begin to feel that he is not smart enough or good enough. Those thoughts will take hold and eventually affect his attitude.

I have come to the conclusion that whatever we set our minds to eventually becomes our lifestyle. When we think positively about ourselves and about life, it is easier to put a foot forward. When we think that nothing can change our circumstances, we sit by the pool of opportunity for years and watch others enjoy the experience of better lives.

Attitude adjustment is necessary to unleash. Apostle Paul knew that, and he admonished us to emulate the attitude of Christ, the attitude of humility and total surrender to the will of His Father (Philippians 2:5–8). Would you be willing to humble yourself before your supervisor, knowing that he is in a position to elevate you? In fact, your next promotion or big assignment will match your attitude in your present circumstance.

Our attitude toward life, whether positive or negative, will eventually determine the level of success we can achieve. Positive attitude generates confidence and propels us to put a foot forward. Negative attitude paralyzes us, cripples us, or causes us to bury our gifts. Negativism begets doubt, low self-esteem, and worry. We worry about things we have not seen and obstacles we have not encountered. Soon our worries take hold of us, and our worries become reality.

Failure may come. We may be pushed down and stepped upon, but we must not stay down; we must get up and move on. What brings us up or keeps us down is our attitude.

When David saw Goliath, he knew Goliath was bigger than him. He knew Goliath could crush him and give his flesh to the birds of the air. But David was confident. He had a positive attitude stemming from the fact that he knew who he was. He had fought with wild animals before and had prevailed. He believed this giant would be like one of them. It was this attitude that spurred his self-confidence and gave him the courage to stand in front of the giant.

When our attitude is positive, we don't see challenges as obstacles. We embrace them as opportunities to unleash our potential. On the other hand, negative attitude breeds fear and loss of focus. It transforms our little hills into huge mountains. We become terrified to even put a foot forward, and then we end up burying our talents.

Money is not everything. That your parents are poor should not be a deterrent. If that were the case, I wouldn't have been able to get here from my humble beginning. It was my attitude that propelled me to want to use my talent, to want to put a foot forward, to want to unleash my potential.

What people think or say should not trouble us. Sometimes people think they know us better than we know ourselves. What matters should be what we think about ourselves. We must think positively and carry ourselves with dignity. It is what we think of ourselves that will determine how we see ourselves and eventually how people see us and think of us.

Cultivating the GSB attitude

a.) **Attitude of gratitude**

Giving thanks brings special joy and satisfaction each time you do it. We must all learn to be grateful for the things we have, no matter how little. When we give thanks for what we have been given, a lot more things will come our way.

When Jesus met the ten lepers outside the city gates, they asked him a favor—to be healed (Luke 17:11–19). Jesus asked them to go and show themselves to the priest. On their way, they found that they had been healed. But only one came back to give thanks. Then something happened—Jesus said to him, "Go, your faith has made you whole."

I attended Methodist College Uzuakoli, and there was a leper colony right by the school. I have seen lepers, and I know firsthand what is involved: the facial distortion, the skin decay, the missing fingers and toes, and the suffering. I met Harcourt White, the master music composer who had also been a leper. His leprosy was gone, but he still had the scars.

So the other nine were healed, but you would still have been able to tell that they once had leprosy. The disease had gone, but the marks would still have been on their faces, fingers, and toes. However, this one who came back to show gratitude was made whole. All the signs of leprosy were gone, and no one could tell that he had once been a leper.

When we cultivate the attitude of gratitude, when we begin to appreciate the little things we have been given, better things come our way. More doors of opportunity open. We fail to see the great things we have because we are busy looking at what others have. Because of this, we fail to show gratitude and appreciation for what we have been given.

When we are tempest tossed, when things are not going right, when life gets tough, when we think that all is lost, all we need to do is count our blessings and give thanks to God. All we have to do is take a moment, focus on the good things we have, and be grateful for them. When we feel grateful, we won't feel envious about someone else's blessings.

When we have an attitude of gratitude, it spreads; everyone around us catches it. Conversely, when our attitude is bad, when we complain and grumble about everything, we tend to scare people away from us. Rather than complain that the roof is leaking, we give thanks because we have a roof over our head. Instead of complaining that you have a menial job, be thankful that you are not at a street corner begging for food. Instead of complaining that your shoes are old and worn, be thankful that you have feet to wear the shoes. Attitude of gratitude will launch us to a new level of opportunity.

b.) **Attitude of servanthood**

We must cultivate the spirit of service with humility, because when we cultivate an attitude of servanthood, it produces kindness and love. It opens doors that otherwise would have remained closed. It creates opportunity for us to put a foot forward and unleash our potential. Jesus Himself said in Matthew 20:27–28 that He came to serve and not to be served. Hence, it is the servanthood attitude that propels us to greater heights and elevates us to positions we never dreamed of. Jesus made this concept practical in John 13:4–15 when he bent down and washed his disciples' feet. At work, at school, and in the community, our humility and service will draw people to us.

Mother Teresa served everyone with humility and love, and she is remembered today by all. She might not have been the richest woman of her time, she might not have been the most beautiful, she might not have been the most eloquent. But she is engraved in the annals of history, and she lives in the hearts of many today, several years after her death, because she served others, the community, and the world. We must humble ourselves enough to be servants to others. To be a servant of the Lord Jesus Christ brings great joy and fulfillment, because when we serve others, we fulfill the commandment of the Lord.

Albert Einstein removed the portraits of two successful people, Isaac Newton and James Maxwell, from his wall and replaced them with those of Mahatma Gandhi and Albert Schweitzer, the replacement of the image of success with the image of service. People are remembered for their services to humanity more than their personal successes.

Promotions come when your boss sees that you are service oriented. Restaurants post toll-free numbers that customers can call to express their feelings and thoughts about the service they received. Car dealerships call after you have taken your car in to ascertain how satisfied you are with the service. They know that customer service is not just everything; it is the only thing. They know that service is not an option for any business; it is critically paramount to the survival of the business.

Service is important to growth, and those who serve receive the reward of growth through promotion, not only at work but in life. Most importantly, the joy and satisfaction that come with knowing that you have served is priceless.

Conversely, when we don't exhibit the attitude of servanthood, we find ourselves always in conflict with people, with our superiors, with society, and those around us see us as arrogant, proud, and selfish. We may not get the promotion we want, and we may forfeit an opportunity to put a foot forward and to unleash our potential.

c.) **Attitude of beatitude**

The Sermon on the Mount recorded in Matthew, chapter 5, is the key to unleashing your potential. Each of the nine beatitudes begins with a blessing, and this blessing will follow anyone who cultivates the attitude of beatitude. The attitudes of being poor in spirit, mourning, meekness, hungering and thirsting after righteousness, mercifulness, purity of heart, peacemaking, persecution for righteousness's sake, tolerance for reviling and gossip, and honesty will control and direct our behavior. It is attitude that will determine whether we put a foot forward or not.

A wealthy man was the CEO of his company. He decided to retire and needed to choose a successor to entrust his company to. He called all his executives and announced that he was about to retire and would choose one of them to be his successor. Of course, each one of them wanted to be the chosen one.

Then he told them that his decision would come at a later date. Meanwhile he gave each one of them a seed and asked them to come back in a year to show how well each had nurtured his seed into a beautiful plant. Perhaps their ability to nurture the seed into a plant would indicate their ability to care for the company.

After the meeting, they all left and apparently began working on their seeds. Every day at work, there were discussions about how well each person's plant was doing.

But one man never said a thing about his plant. The problem was that his seed did not even sprout. He watered and nurtured the seed, but nothing seemed to happen. His wife encouraged him to continue to water. Perhaps, one day, the seed would take root.

For several months, nothing happened. The day came when everyone had to present their plants to the CEO for his decision. This man did not want to go to that ceremony because he had nothing to present. His wife encouraged him to take the pot and show his boss that he had indeed planted the seed but nothing had happened. The young man reluctantly agreed.

When the time came, everyone brought out their plants and exhibited them on pedestals. The plants were beautiful. The CEO walked around inspecting the plants. His eyes caught a pot filled with potting soil but no plant. He asked who had brought the pot.

Suppressed laughter from the others swept the auditorium. The young man raised his hand, and the CEO invited him to the podium. When he put his foot forward on the podium, the CEO announced to all the people, "Ladies and gentlemen, this is your new CEO!"

Everyone marveled, including the young man. The retiring CEO said, "I gave each one of you a seed, but what you didn't know was that all the seeds had been half boiled and therefore could not grow. This young man was honest. The rest of you bought similar seeds and planted them when you saw that the one I gave you was not sprouting."

I watched a story on television about a homeless man who returned a diamond ring to a woman who accidentally dropped it in the man's begging bowl. For many months, this homeless man had sat on the street corner, begging for change. One day, among the pennies and nickels and dimes he had collected, he found a diamond engagement ring in his cup. He took the ring to a jewelry store for appraisal. They offered to give him $4,000 for it.

He quickly realized that the ring must be worth much more than the amount they offered him. Instead of selling the ring and making a fortune, or at least getting off the streets, he decided to return it. But he didn't know who the owner was.

He went back to the spot where he got the ring, in the event the owner returned looking for it. And that's what happened. The lady who had lost the ring returned, and the homeless man handed her the ring. Then something happened—people heard about this rare gesture by the homeless man, and donations poured in like rain for him. He was no longer homeless.

All he did was put a foot forward; all he did was show an act of kindness. The rest is history. His blessings flowed!

This was a homeless man who scrounged for pennies every day to buy hamburger, yet he returned a ring worth more than $4,000. When asked what made him return the ring, he gave credit to his father, who taught him to always be honest.

His father hadn't taught him how to get rich; riches will come and go. He hadn't taught him how to amass wealth; wealth will come and go. The man's father left him with priceless gifts: the gift of honesty even in abject poverty, the gift of meekness even in weakness, and the gift of humility even in the face of adversity. These were gifts that endured. What a lesson on teaching a child the way he should go!

The blessing is for the poor in spirit, the humble, and the brokenhearted, for theirs is the kingdom of heaven. The kingdom is not for the pompous, the arrogant, and the proud; it is for those who serve. It is for those who are willing to surrender their egos even when they know they are right.

The blessing is for those who mourn, those who may have made mistakes in the past and are saddened and troubled by those mistakes, and those who repent for their failures, for they shall be comforted.

The blessing is for the meek, those who are humble, gentle, and kind, those who endure, and those who are ready to give of themselves for the unity of their family and group. These shall inherit the earth. Wherever the soles of their feet shall touch will be their inheritance.

The blessing is for those who hunger and thirst after righteousness, those who accept their guilt and inability to control their impulses, and those who realize that they are born in sin. These shall be filled.

The blessing is for the merciful, those who are unselfish, compassionate, considerate, forgiving, and kind. These shall obtain mercy.

The blessing is for the pure in heart, those who are without envy or jealousy, those who forgive others who trespass against them, those whose thoughts and feelings are devoid of stain, and those whose actions and character are blameless. These shall see God.

The blessing is for the peacemakers, those who believe in doing unto others as they would want others to do unto them, those who love without condition and forgive seventy times seven, those who turn the other cheek to be slapped, and those who seek peace with all their might. These shall be called the children of God.

The blessing is for those who are persecuted for righteousness's sake, those whose lights shine so that men see their good works and glorify their Father who is in heaven, and those who discover and are not afraid to use their gifts, even when they are ridiculed and oppressed because of the love they share. The kingdom of God belongs to these.

The blessing is for those who are reviled, persecuted, and gossiped falsely about by men; and those who are ready to take up the cross and follow Jesus, knowing that they will be ridiculed, oppressed, harassed, and troubled in the process. These shall receive not only exceeding joy and gladness on earth, but a great reward in heaven.

Once we realize that the kingdom of God is within us, we will understand that our advancement and our ability to put a foot forward are within us. Unleashing our potential is dependent on our attitude toward ourselves, others, and life as a whole. There is nothing we can do of our own strength; we must see ourselves as totally dependent on God. We must believe that we can do all things through Christ who strengthens us.

Skill

Every one of us has a unique gift, and it is in this gift that our skills are most pronounced. The ease with which we perform complex tasks and acquire new skills in certain areas of expertise should alert us to our potential and motivate us to put a foot forward and unleash that expertise. Actors and actresses take on new roles and excel instantly because they have discovered their abilities. Prior experience elicits confidence and reduces fright. Once we put a foot forward, we will begin to acquire new skills and eventually develop the confidence to unleash our potential at a more complex level.

Nothing good comes easy, they say. Skill is acquired over a long period of time. To acquire the skills necessary to be successful takes patience and practice. In order to achieve and maintain a competitive edge, teachers must continue to attend in-service training. Athletes must put in hours of practice every day. Doctors must attend conferences and read research journals. There is no maximum level of skill that you can attain. Whatever your gift is, you must continue to develop it in order to excel in it. An undeveloped skill is a buried gift.

Honesty

Self-deceit is a killer. You must be honest with yourself. You shouldn't want to be something only because your friends are that.

If you are not sure of your gift yet, I encourage you to look into your BACKPACK. You may well discover your hidden gift. Millions of contestants appear on the *American Idol* stage for auditions each season. There are those who come because they know in all honesty that they can sing. There are also those who have never practiced singing even in the shower, and they appear in borrowed robes. The reaction of the judges sometimes gives a hint of what I mean here.

However, those who have discovered their gifts don't hesitate to put a foot forward. It does not matter what the judges think or how many times those contestants have been rejected; they continue to unleash. They are confident because they know the truth, and they are honest with themselves.

I have seen parents push their children to become who they are not. The children simply go along with it to please their parents.

As a professor, I have watched as students come in from high school and declare premed majors. Two semesters into it, they change to nursing. Two years into that career path, they change again to teaching. I've spent time with some of them, and I discovered that they had no interest in the sciences in the first place. Their grades in the sciences in high school were nothing to write home about, and their explanations for switching majors were always the same: "My parents wanted me to major in medicine." "I really don't want to be here!" "I don't want to do this."

Upon graduating with a degree in education, most of these students have gone on to become great teachers, instructional coordinators, assistant principals, and principals.

Honesty has always been and will always be the best policy when you want to put your foot forward and unleash your potential. Understand who you are. Identify your gift, and then have the confidence to unleash.

8

You Must Connect to Unleash

We have seen how important our attitude is in reaching our goals and achieving our dreams. Negative attitude will alienate us from people and cost us good friends. We all need good people around us. No one can thrive in isolation. We need our family members. We need our neighbors; we need our coworkers. We must work hard to keep good friends, good people, and good neighbors, and be at peace with our families. We need each other.

The lame man at the pool of Bethesda sat there for many years with no one to help him. People might have passed by him as they jumped in the pool. Some might have jumped over him. No one cared to help him get in the water.

They all knew he needed that help. Could it be that the lame man didn't have friends or family members? Why didn't he have anybody to help him? When he got his healing, he picked up his bed and ran off. Where was he running off to? Who was he running off to meet? Could it be that he had a family after all? Perhaps because he was crippled and thus an unproductive family member, everyone left him to suffer alone. What were their reactions when they saw him?

The homeless man who returned the engagement ring and changed his life spent years on winter-cold streets, begging for money. No one seemed to care about him. It appeared he had no family and no friends. Then he showed an act of kindness, and his life changed. Suddenly he had more friends than he ever imagined. Where were they while he was out in the cold?

There was a man who disconnected himself from his wife, his children, his friends, and even his community. He moved into an efficiency apartment, where he lived in isolation. He was a cab driver, but he didn't want to have anything to do with anybody.

No one knew when he got sick. It was the pungent odor emanating from his apartment that drew the attention of his neighbors. They called the police, and when the apartment was forced open, they found his decaying body on the floor. He had died ten days prior. What a sad way to die!

Good connections are priceless. If you are a freshman in college, you must connect with people to make your campus experience less stressful. You must also choose carefully whom you connect with. Bad connections can pull you down. Choose friends who will lift you up, friends with whom you can share ideas, friends with similar interests, goals, and aspirations.

Keeping good friends is a product of our positive attitude, our humility, and our honesty. No one is an island, it has been said. We need each other at some point in our lives. If you were sitting by your pool of Bethesda, crippled by sickness, poverty, hopelessness, and helplessness, would you have friends who would put you in the pool so you could get healed, get help? If you don't have such friends, why not? Could it be something about you that drives people away? Could it be your arrogance, obnoxious attitude, and pride? You must be connected to unleash your potential.

We cannot expect to have perfect friends. After all, we are not perfect. No human being is perfect. The man who was paralyzed could not have been perfect. He must have wronged his friends at one time or the other. But he had friends who were forgiving in spirit, friends who were loyal and committed to the relationship, and friends who would not hold grudges. If we expect people to accept us the way we are, we must equally be willing to accept others the way they are. If we expect to have good friends, we must be good friends to others.

We should be able to connect with unselfish people who are willing to alert us when they hear of new business or career opportunities. These people will help us when we need it to put a foot forward. Success comes with its failures, but we need to connect with people, friends, and family who will pick us up, hold us up, and possibly bring us to our place of blessing, even if it means tearing the roof.

I had a very close relationship with my sister, even from childhood. We had our sibling times, but we always made up quickly. My father had told me that I would go to America someday, get a good education, and become a doctor and a professor. To be honest with you, I didn't know how that would come to pass, but I believed.

Years later, my sister got married and went to the United States. Because of the love we had for each other, and because we were connected, she did everything she could to make sure that I came to the United States. And I did!

About six years after I came, I still did not have a green card. I was paying foreign student tuition to attend college, which cost an arm and a leg. I needed to become a resident in order to make my life easier and better.

I worked full-time at a restaurant in order to pay the foreign student tuition. I came to class late one day, and my professor wanted to know why. I explained that I had worked the evening shift the previous day and got off at four o'clock that morning. I sat on the couch to rest for an hour or two before getting ready for school. As I was watching the television, I fell asleep. When I opened my eyes again, it was almost ten o'clock, and my class started at ten. I scampered off the couch, and by the time I got to class, the session was almost over.

He told me what a good student I was, how he had been watching my behavior since I enrolled in that class, how respectful and courteous I had been, and so on. It was out of character for me to come to class late, he said. What he didn't quite know was that in my culture growing up, students didn't speak until the teacher asked them to speak. Students didn't disrespect teachers. Students had to be seated before the teacher entered the classroom. Students didn't disrupt class. All that interested him, and he wanted to know more about me.

We became friends despite the fact that he was my professor. He would invite me to his office, and we would talk about life in Nigeria and how it compared with life here in America.

As we were talking after class one day, he told me that his uncle, who was in his sixties then, wanted to do business in Nigeria. The professor wanted to know if I had any connections at home to facilitate this endeavor.

By then, I had been away from my country for quite some time, and I didn't know if the people I knew there would be interested. I promised him I would try. But before we could complete the process, his uncle changed his mind.

Still, we kept in touch. We talked on the phone once in a while. One day, he asked me to meet him at a restaurant for lunch. I did. His nephew had told him that I paid foreign student tuition, and the professor invited me to go with him to meet his attorney. We did, and I found out that I was qualified to receive amnesty. His attorney processed my papers and submitted them at no charge to me, and that was how I got my green card.

I was sitting by the pool of Bethesda, and the angel of the Lord had stirred the waters. I had a friend who helped me get into the water, and the rest is history. I was connected with good people, people who lifted me up rather than pulled me down. Perhaps such good fortune would have eluded me had the professor found me to be disrespectful or arrogant or prideful. It would have eluded me if I had been lazy and nonchalant.

In order to unleash your potential, you must make connections with people. You must remain on good terms with everyone, including your family members. That will come only when you are willing to forgive, be at peace, and be meek, gentle, humble, and honest. We all need human connections if we want to put a foot forward and achieve our goals. We must connect with those who love us just the way we are.

The paralyzed man could not help himself (Luke 5:17–25). He could not walk. He could not even put a foot forward. Though he was in that state, he was connected with good people. Perhaps he was good to them before he got so sick. He must have been friendly and humble. He must have shared what he had with them. They must have spent time together. They were connected, so when he got sick, his connections remained intact.

How many people lose their friends because they become seriously sick or poor? Their friends abandoned them when they needed help the most. Not so with this man. His friends came to his rescue.

They knew Jesus was in town, and they had heard that He was the great Physician who could cure all manner of diseases. They quickly went to the paralyzed man, picked him up in his bed, and rushed him to where Jesus was.

But there was a problem. The crowd was too big, and they could not get their friend through to Jesus. They went up the housetop, tore off the roof, and lowered him to Jesus's feet.

What a group! They cared so much about their friend that they were willing to break someone else's roof. All they wanted was for their friend to be healed. (I am sure they paid the homeowner later for his repairs.)

Listen to this: Jesus healed the paralyzed man because of the faith of his friends (Luke 5:20). Don't we all need such friends? We must stay connected to unleash our potential.

9

Your Gift Is in Your BACKPACK

In your BACKPACK, you will find your unique gift. The BACKPACK concept is a framework to help us understand who we are and the perspective of others. The idea stems from the fact that every individual carries a backpack—though perhaps, if you are no longer a student, that "backpack" takes the form of a purse, a briefcase, or a tool belt—and each backpack contains a constellation of personal items that are of interest and unique to the individual. It is this understanding that affords us the opportunity to determine what our gifts are and how to develop the skills needed to unleash our potential.

A preacher must have working knowledge of his congregation in order to be a good shepherd. A furniture maker must have a working knowledge of the grain of the wood in order to create fine furniture. An employer must understand his employees in order to create a productive working environment. Workers must know their colleagues in order to have a friendly atmosphere in the workplace. Parents must understand their children in order to properly direct them. Teachers must understand their students in order to align their teaching style with the learning styles of their students.

Backpacks come in different colors, sizes, shapes, and materials, made by different manufacturers in different parts of the world. As there are similarities and differences in the outward appearance of the backpacks, there are similarities and differences among their contents.

In each person's identity is stored unique social characteristics related to a variety of factors. The BACKPACK acronym spells:

- background
- ability
- cultural orientation
- knowledge
- personality
- attitude
- communication pattern
- keep

Everything we do is a reflection of our BACKPACKs, a cultural script written, produced, and directed by culture bearers—parents, relatives, teachers, and the community. This creates the unique qualities and varying lifestyles of the people around us.

Ignoring the contents of our BACKPACKs may cause us to miss our purpose and deprive us of the opportunity to channel our strength in the direction of our talents. Understanding our BACKPACKs constitutes essential preparation for facilitating, structuring, and validating our readiness to perform. We must use our knowledge of our BACKPACKs to identify our strengths and weaknesses, identify our interests and needs, increase our creativity and effectiveness, and enhance our relationships with others.

Background

We all have different needs and interests and come from different economic and social backgrounds. This affects the way we perceive our world and our ability to take that STEP. Some of us come from upper-class households while others come from middle- or lower-class households. In some families, both parents are educated; in some, one parent is educated; in others, neither parent is educated. Some are poor; some are rich. Some have traveled; some have not gone beyond their neighborhoods. Some come from stable, functional families; some come from unstable homes and are constantly moving from place to place.

Some families are dysfunctional due to divorce and other issues. Some of us come from homes with deep family tragedies, where we have been exposed to drugs even at an early age. Some have parents who are interested in school; some have parents who couldn't care less. Some of us are physically, emotionally, and mentally abused.

These differences imply that there are some of us who are crippled by these realities. Harsh experience has prevented us from putting a foot forward and from unleashing our potential. But we must arise; we must shake off the dust of blame and confusion. We must take up our beds, and we must walk. We must tap into our backgrounds, our environments, our circles of influence.

When I was a little boy, I loved to listen to tales in the moonlight. I still remember most of the stories I heard then. Now, I am able to tell my own story because I had the inspiration and motivation to do so.

I will never forget when, in elementary school, our teacher asked us to draw a car. There was a boy, Chima, whose parents were well-to-do. He had been brought to the village to attend school in order to have the village experience. Chima's rendition of a car was spectacular in our eyes, probably because we hadn't paid attention to cars; only one or two drove past us once in a while. But because Chima had ridden in one in the city, he was able to do a better job than those of us who had merely caught a glimpse of a car from a distance.

However, when the teacher asked us to draw a goat, boy, come and see! My drawing of a goat was breathtakingly detailed, while Chima's rendition of a goat looked more like a car. That was the background factor.

Bill Gates and Paul Allen were able to work on computers and discovered they had a wonderful talent. I wonder what would have happened if they had been born and raised in some third world country where there were no computers to mess with. Perhaps Mr. Gates would have completed his university education.

When David came to the camp to face Goliath, he tapped into his background—his experience as a little shepherd boy. He recited how he had killed the lions and bears that came to attack his sheep. That background gave him the assurance that he had the potential to do greater things. When he saw the giant in front of him, he was not intimidated. He put a foot forward and unleashed that potential. Then something happened—the giant came crashing down.

Ability

We all have varied ability levels: different skills and abilities, strengths and weaknesses. We must capitalize on our strengths and interests to determine our goals and aspirations.

You do not have to be a five-talent person to put a foot forward. You may not discover your abilities until you have unleashed your potential. You are reading this book because I decided to arise, take up my pen, and write. It does not matter the foot I put forward first. What matters is that I started.

As a teacher, I discovered that many parents, especially in primary schools, try to help their children with their homework. By so doing, the parents deprive the children of the ability to unleash their potential. I have seen students' science projects, and I have always known which child did what. Some parents start and complete the projects, and all that those children did was display the results for viewing. The students may make good grades in that science project, but that doesn't represent their ability.

The story of a butterfly in a cocoon is a good example. I have used it quite often while preparing student teachers. The caterpillar crawls into the cocoon, goes through a process of metamorphosis, transforms into a beautiful butterfly, and is ready to come out of the shell. The butterfly has to push its way out of the cocoon, and while it is doing so, blood begins to circulate through the wings and all over its body, making it stronger and ready to face the world outside. Hence, when the butterfly comes out of the cocoon, it can fly!

However, if someone cuts the cocoon for the butterfly and helps it to come out, the butterfly will indeed come out. It will look like a butterfly. But it will not be able to fly.

This is why you find people who have graduated from school but cannot function in their areas of expertise.

Most parents want their children to be medical doctors, engineers, and other highly paid professionals. But the parents have not taken the time to look at their children's report cards to see where their strengths lie.

You will discover your gift by discovering your ability.

There is absolutely nothing wrong with pushing children to become doctors and engineers, but such decisions must be made with pristine clarity of understanding of what children are capable of doing. It would be interesting to see what would happen in a city where every resident is a medical doctor and the air conditioning system breaks down in the heat of the summer or a sewage pipe explodes.

Cultural orientation

Each culture views the world from a different perspective, and culture greatly influences our identities. What we have learned from our culture helps us define and direct our interpretation of the environment and the world. Our identities, thoughts, characters, and feelings are all culturally scripted.

As a child, my friends and I made musical instruments from bamboo stems. We would sing as we wove baskets and made beads with locally found objects. It was by playing this way that my artistic talent came alive. I discovered that I could paint, sculpt, carve, sing, and dance.

As I stated earlier, in my birth culture, teachers were highly respected. They were said to be the custodians of knowledge, wisdom, and intelligence. Every parent wished to have a child who would become a teacher. Mothers sent fruit to teachers. Teachers received gifts of fresh vegetables. On the day a teacher visited a family, everything was cleaned; the best soup was cooked. Everyone admired teachers. I wanted to become a teacher.

Knowledge

We all bring to our world a cultural script or knowledge gained through experience from interaction with our environment. Tapping this knowledge is essential for creativity to flourish. We learn most effectively when we match activities to our prior knowledge and interests, and when we build on what we already know and can do. In other words, nothing is learned in isolation. Our prior knowledge must serve as a prerequisite for new learning.

We must know what already exists in order to create something new. The most creative problems are those that motivate us to use the skills and knowledge we already have and to seek more if needed. A person cannot wake up in the morning and decide to become an expert in some field of knowledge that he has no idea exists.

Before you decide on a major in college, before you put a foot forward, before you unleash, look back into your BACKPACK. What is in your high school transcript? What knowledge base are you taking with you? Employers often ask for experience when someone applies for a job. What they are actually looking for is your background, ability, and knowledge in the area of interest. Educated as a teacher, why would I even apply for a job as an engineer?

Personality

Our personalities are characterized by the way we behave and carry ourselves. This comes as a result of accumulation of past experiences and our cultural script. It also stems from our life experiences and the contents of our BACKPACK. Our determination, commitment, enthusiasm, and dedication are aspects of our personalities that tilt us and cause us to want to put a foot forward and unleash our potential. Peter was bold even when others were too shy or afraid to step out of the boat. When we are positive and are willing to get along with others, when we are cooperative and patient and willing to try new things, we find that success is limitless; all we have to do is recognize the opportunity.

Our personalities are often influenced by our cultural orientation. I come from a culture where respect, saving face, filial piety, family orientation, and obedience are highly valued norms. Our parents taught my siblings and I good social relationships and to conduct ourselves in ways that would not bring shame to the family. We are often humble and sometimes overly shy, dependent, or introverted. We tend to enjoy working in groups rather than as individuals.

In American culture, on the other hand, high value is placed on self-reliance, competition, and individual achievement. Most folks here are autonomous, independent, outgoing, and extroverted.

Our individual personalities depend very much on self-image and personal identity. We may experience difficulties or cultural clashes in our day-to-day interactions with others if we do not understand how our cultural orientation influences our personalities, self-awareness, and self-concepts.

Attitude

Each culture embodies a set of beliefs and practices that influence knowledge seeking, socialization, and patterns of coping with the environment. These cultural beliefs and practices often influence our attitudes toward every aspect of life. It is important that we understand our belief systems, ontological values, and cultural orientations in order to make informed decisions and unleash our potential.

Because I grew up where teachers are highly respected, my attitude toward teachers is positive. I view teachers as people with authority. I would not question their directives. On the other hand, if someone has grown up in an environment where teachers are treated poorly, that person may not hesitate to contradict a teacher and question the reasoning behind his directives.

Behaviors that appear unacceptable in one culture may be acceptable in another. When we understand this concept, it creates a window through which we see others from different viewpoints, enhance our understanding of and interaction with them.

Communication pattern

Different cultures have different patterns of communication. Our communication styles are shaped by our cultures and ethnicities.

Every culture communicates with symbols, and differences in the interpretation of those symbols lead to either successful or unsuccessful communication between people from different cultures. Symbols bind people together, but they can likewise separate people who do not share the same interpretations.

We bring to our workplaces and social lives various modes of communication based on our home cultural orientations. These cultural norms of the home may conflict with the cultural norms of others with devastating consequences.

Speaking a different language should not be a handicap; it should be an asset to be cultivated and encouraged. We must be careful to not ridicule, invalidate, or demoralize people because of their linguistic differences.

Keep

Keep refers to readiness and poise. It gives us an edge in gaining trust, responsibility, and advancement. It refers to our interests and appearance. It is about those things we love to collect and keep. As a young boy, Bill Gates loved to work with computers. He collected and kept anything he could find that related to them. Most of the time, we discover our gifts and passions from those little things that always catch our eyes and tickle our fancies; those things we collect and keep.

Keep also refers to our outward appearance, self-maintenance, physical, emotional, and mental health, and personal hygiene. It is a reflection of our home environment and our attitude toward self. Our appearance communicates our respect and pride for what we do.

Our appearance and the way we carry ourselves reflect our understanding of the demands of our professions and the value we ascribe to them.

10

Put Any *Fruit* Forward

As a little boy, I enjoyed different kinds of fruits. I could climb up the tree, pluck them out personally, and eat as much as I wanted. There was a mango tree in our compound, as well as guava, paw-paw, coconut, pear, orange, and many others, and I enjoyed each one of them in their seasons.

There was something fascinating about these fruits. To get to the seed, you had to bite or peel through layers of skin. The seeds were well protected and universally recognized. Hand carried from one region or country to another, they thrived and produced fruit. I wasn't very surprised that I came to the United States and found these fruits. Even when I stopped over in London, I saw them. I saw them in France. My friend in Saudi Arabia told me they were there. Fruit seeds have unrestricted access to anywhere in the world, perhaps with multiple entry visas.

The same is not true about some plants or flowers whose seeds are on the surface, exposed to the birds of the air and natural elements. Most of these seeds are localized. In other words, they can only thrive in their region of origin. They bloom only for a season, and they die. The Texas bluebonnet is a beautiful flower and the state flower, but it is recognized as such only in Texas. Alaskan forget-me-not is local to Alaska, and so are other states' flowers.

You can decide to be a localized seed that can only thrive in your neighborhood, or you may choose to package yourself in such a way that you can thrive and bear fruit anywhere in the world. It is your training and preparation that will sustain you and catapult you to greater heights regardless of where you may find yourself.

If you want to be a teacher, prepare yourself so that you can teach anywhere in the world. If you want to be a doctor, prepare yourself so you can practice anywhere in the world. Why would you settle for just enough training to teach only the children in the neighborhood where you grew up?

Making the right choices is essential before putting a foot forward.

- *Celery (Salary):* In determining your gift, don't make the paycheck your driving force. Money is good, but it must not be the reason you want to choose a career. It must not be the reason that you want to unleash your potential. Don't go to work because you will be receiving a reward, a salary. Don't go to work because you will be punished if you don't, or because you need money to pay your bills. You could make money doing a lot of other things. Rather, come to work because you are passionate about what you do. Your creativity, skill, and talent come alive more when you feel motivated from within by an inner drive. It is the gift in you that must drive you to put a foot forward. Your passion must outweigh your desire to get a paycheck. Find your gift, prepare yourself, and all other things will follow.
- *Lettuce ("Let us"):* I have always heard people say that no one is an island. At work, at school, in your neighborhood, or in your community, you must work with others to make yourself even better. You must be a team player. You must be able to get along. You cannot work well with only your own folks. The world is a multicultural, pluralistic society, and it gets smaller by the day. We must learn to live together, work together, and play together. "Lettuce" work together! "Lettuce" live together! "Lettuce" get along!
- *Onions ("Own yours"):* Normally in a group assignment, only a few people do most of the task. You have to always be yourself and not allow others to discourage you. To be successful in a group setting, you must own your aspect of the task. Your team is depending on you to come through. They know you are

capable, and you must be reliable, available, dependable, and accountable. In other words, you must take ownership of your piece of the pie.

- *Carrot ("Carry out"):* "Carrot" your assigned duties and responsibilities diligently. If you commit to it, do it! Do not accept what you know you can't do. Lip service is a big destroyer. You alone know what your abilities are. It is better that you decline than accept and not perform.

- *Cantaloupe ("Can't elope"):* You "cantaloupe" from your responsibilities. When the going gets tough, most people want to quit. Quitting is not the solution to any problem. When you make a mistake, learn from it. When you fall down, get up and move on. Don't create an excuse to quit a job or quit school or quit a relationship. Work it out! You can't just elope.

- *Cherry ("Cherish"):* Cherish the opportunity you have and give it your best. There are people who are not as fortunate as you are. You are where you are because you have put a foot forward and unleashed your potential. One of the reasons we don't appreciate what we have is because we are busy focusing on what others have. We are more concerned about what we don't have. Remember that success is not about where you are; it is about the struggles you had to overcome to get there. Have a positive attitude. Enjoy what you have. Cherish the opportunity. Why would you complain that you don't have good shoes when there are others who don't have feet to wear shoes?

- *Potato ("Put off to"):* Don't "potato" tomorrow that which you can accomplish today. When we procrastinate, it creates a pile of obligations that becomes overwhelming and stressful. In other words, don't be lazy! Is there a job application that you need to complete and send out? Complete it now. Is there a career that you have been thinking about pursuing but haven't started? Start now. Is there a needy neighbor whom you have always wanted to help, but you have been putting it off? Help him now. "Arise, take up your bed, and walk!" The response of faith was immediate.

- *Squash:* You must not be a part of gossip. When you encounter gossip, squash it right there. Kill it before you entangle yourself in a web of mess. The tongue is like an old shoelace; if not held down it will flap around uncontrollably. Gossip has cost people good jobs, good friendships, good opportunities, and good connections. Stop it before it stops you.

- *Pear ("Pair"):* Pair up with someone—a classmate, a colleague, a good friend. Collaborate and share ideas. If you are a student, find a good study mate, a good friend, but choose wisely. If you are a professional, find a buddy you can run ideas by. Critique each other and share knowledge and experience. I hear people say that iron sharpens iron, and I believe it. You cannot be effective by working alone all the time. However, you must be careful to avoid distractions.

  When Peter and John met the lame man at the Beautiful gate, a very interesting set of events took place. Peter paired up with John, and they were going to the temple to pray. When the lame man saw them, he asked them for money (Acts 3:1–9). First, Peter said to the lame man, "Look at us." The lame man looked at them intently, hoping to get some money from them. Then Peter said to the lame man, "Silver or gold have I not, but what I have I'll give to you." Notice that Peter suddenly switched from plural to singular. He was no longer speaking about "us"; he was speaking about himself.

  Why didn't he continue with "Silver or gold have we not?" Why did he change to "Silver or gold have I not?" Many people might have been watching them interact with the lame man. John might have been distracted. Peter quickly realized that, and he disengaged himself momentarily from John in order to accomplish the task at hand. He did that, and both continued on their journey to the temple.

- *Orange ("Arrange"):* Arrange your priorities. Stay on task. Don't try to do too much at a time. Maintain focus and know what goal you have set your mind to accomplish. Avoid distractions. Work on your tasks one step at a time, one day at a time.

- *Apple ("Apply"):* Apply wisdom always. Don't make irrational decisions or take unnecessary actions. Make wise choices. Do not allow your body to rule your mind. Exercise control. You don't have to do it (whatever "it" may be) just because everyone else is doing it.
- *Avocado ("Avail can do"):* I've always asked myself, "Avail can do?" In other words, "Am I available and can do whatever it is that I have been assigned?" Some people are available, but they cannot do the job. Others can do the job, but they are not available. Success is capability and availability.
- *Tulip ("Tie up your lip"):* If you have nothing positive to say about someone, *hush*! Enough said.
- *Mango ("Man go"):* It is always in your best interest to let the man go—or the woman go, as the case may be. In other words, you must learn to forgive. Release people. Remember that you cannot go forward if you are entangled with someone, and you cannot stand up when you are holding someone on the ground. Let the man go!
- *Olive ("Or leave"):* Love it or leave it. Don't come to work because you feel you have to. Come because you love what you do. If you don't think it is what you want to do, please leave. Staying there will hurt everyone, including, of course, yourself. You may not like that you are a waiter at a restaurant or a cashier at a fast-food eatery, but you took the job in the first place, so cheer up. Don't scare away customers with your obnoxious attitude. If you don't enjoy working with the public, then don't work with the public. If you are a police officer, a doctor, a nurse, a teacher—love it or leave. Remember, you can't take a job because of the "celery."
- *Tomatoes ("To my toes"):* Always remind yourself to bend to your toes. Find time to touch them every day. In other words, *exercise*. Find time to stay fit and healthy.
- *Peas ("Peace"):* Always be at peace with yourself and everyone.

11

Unlock that PADLOCK
to Unleash

Before you can put a foot forward, you must have the right key to unlock your PADLOCK.

There are seven keys: you must *position* yourself, you must make necessary *adjustments*, you must *deal* with your fears, you must *locate* your opportunity, you must be *optimistic*, you must *cultivate* your gift, and you must *keep* an open mind.

Position yourself

Positioning yourself requires humility. When Zacchaeus heard that Jesus of Nazareth was scheduled to pass through his city, he did something remarkable. Zacchaeus had heard about Jesus: how He made the blind to see, how He made the lame to walk, and how He healed the woman with the issue of blood. Zacchaeus wanted to see this Man who had inspired his colleague, Matthew, to leave everything and follow Him.

So Zacchaeus climbed a sycamore tree (Luke 19:1–10). He recognized the opportunity, and he was aware of his shortcomings. He was a short man, and he figured that he would not be able to see Jesus because of this challenge. Instead of sitting at home and complaining about his height disadvantage, perhaps blaming his parents and God for making him short, he made the decision to go forth. He positioned himself.

Zacchaeus was a rich man, probably the head of the tax collectors. He had all he needed and wanted. Ordinarily, pride wouldn't let him do what he did. He had to humble himself to do it. Then Jesus sought him out, and his life changed. His humility positioned him.

Positioning yourself requires obedience. David went to the camp of the Israelites, where Goliath was taunting the people of God (1 Samuel 17). Obedience took David there. His father asked him to take food to his brothers in the battlefield. He obeyed. He could have refused. He could have stayed in the wilderness, and no one would have bothered him. He chose to go to the camp in obedience to his father. He positioned himself, and God used him to His glory. David didn't hide himself behind a tent. He asked some of the soldiers, "What will be done for the man who kills this Philistine?" (1 Samuel 17:26). Even the pressure from his big brother, Eliab, didn't intimidate him.

David encouraged Saul the king to be of good cheer. While he was in the presence of King Saul, he didn't hesitate to present his résumé to the king.

> Your servant has been keeping his father's sheep. When a lion or a bear came and carried off a sheep from the flock, I went after it, struck it and rescued the sheep from its mouth. When it turned on me, I seized it by its hair, struck it and killed it. Your servant has killed both the lion and the bear; this uncircumcised Philistine will be like one of them, because he has defied the armies of the living God. The LORD who rescued me from the paw of the lion and the paw of the bear will rescue me from the hand of this Philistine. (1 Samuel 17:34–37)

David's obedience positioned him to unleash his potential.

Joseph knew his brothers hated him, but at his father's request, he agreed to take food to them in Shechem (Genesis 37:13–36). It was his obedience that positioned him to live out his dream. His brothers put him in a dry pit and finally sold him to a company of Ishmaelites from Gilead. The Ishmaelites took Joseph to Egypt. There, he lived his dream. What would have happened to Joseph's dream if he had refused to obey his father? What would have happened if he had given up when he didn't find his brothers at first? What would have happened if he had been afraid of the unknown? It is when obedience is fulfilled that the promise is made manifest.

Positioning yourself requires sacrifice. Queen Esther knew what was at stake when she took the decision to position herself. She was the queen, and she had servants and everything she needed, including the promise of half the kingdom at her request (Esther 5:3). She sacrificed all of these and committed herself to doing whatever it took to save her people, stating, "I will go to the king, even though it is against the law, And if I perish, I perish" (Esther 4:16). Was Esther afraid? Of course she was. Did she think she might lose her life? Of course she did. But did all that intimidate her? Not at all! She was willing to make that sacrifice.

Positioning yourself requires self-determination. While Moses was keeping the flock of his father-in-law, he led the flock to the back side of the desert and came to the mountain of God (Exodus 3:1). Moses was diligently doing his work. It was not his sheep that he was keeping. They were someone else's, but he was shepherding them to the best of his ability. Then he led them to the mountain of God. Talk about positioning!

It was there that the angel of the Lord appeared to him in a flame of fire. Notice what Moses did; he turned aside to see this great sight (Exodus 3:3). He did not ignore it. He didn't observe it from a distance. He moved up to it. And something happened. When God saw that Moses had turned aside to see, that he had positioned himself, God called him, introduced Himself, and gave Moses the promotion—like God to Pharaoh (Exodus 7:1).

Positioning yourself requires honesty. Recall that young CEO we saw in chapter 7. While others were busy trying to fake their way to the top, he remained honest. He didn't want to cheat like the others did. At the end of the day, his honesty paid off. To the chagrin of his colleagues, he was appointed the CEO of the company.

Let's go back to the homeless man who returned the expensive engagement ring. He could have pawned it and used the money to rent an apartment. He could have used the money to provide food for himself. There was a lot he could have done with the money, but he chose to be honest. He positioned himself, and his reward was far better than he had ever imagined.

Positioning yourself requires preparedness. Opportunities have a way of popping up on us. If we are not prepared or are ill-prepared, we will lose the opportunity or maybe not function well in it. We don't have to be totally prepared, but we must continue to strive for excellence.

There is a gift in you, a unique gift. One thing is to discover your gift; the other is to develop it. Preparedness involves continually acquiring skills beyond your unique gift.

If an educated person is defined as one who knows something about everything and everything about something, then no one is educated. Not one! This is evident in the way universities prepare their students. Every student who enters a university, regardless of major, must take the university's core courses. You are then required to take more courses in your area of specialization, and then electives, some of which may not be related to your major field of study.

The university's goal is to produce educated people, and the process begins when you get in. In other words, if your major is biology, you are nevertheless required to take history, government, sociology, mathematics, English, and so on. These requirements are an attempt to teach you something about everything.

Then you are required to take several courses in biology, so that you start working toward knowing everything about your chosen specialty. After graduation, you are expected to continue to acquire knowledge. That is why the graduation ceremony is called *commencement*. It is only the beginning.

So if you are biology major, you begin to learn everything there is to know about biology. You are also required to know something about everything else. But there is no end point to that educational process. We must continue to strive for excellence.

Moses, somehow, felt he would be the one to lead the Israelites out of bondage. He wasn't quite ready to undertake that herculean task, and he delved into it ill-prepared. It didn't work. He fled, and for forty years, he underwent rigorous training and skill development. Among other things, he first had to learn to lead the sheep.

Positioning yourself includes:

- *Professional ethics:* You must always exhibit honesty and confidentiality. Your friends, colleagues, immediate supervisors, subordinates, and family members must be able to trust you.
- *Professional appearance:* Your professional appearance communicates your preparedness, your attitude toward your profession, and your respect and pride for what you do. You must always dress appropriately as your duty demands.
- *Professional demeanor and responsibility:* Your poise and the way you comport yourself reflect your understanding of the demands of your profession. You must be dependable and complete your assigned tasks on time. *Tardiness* and *unnecessary absence* should not be in your vocabulary. Your interaction with your supervisors, staff, and colleagues must be effective. Bursts of anger must have no place. Whatever you find yourself doing, give it your best because people are watching.
- *Emotional maturity:* Your current assignment may come with frustrations and stress, but you must learn to deal with them and respond to them appropriately.
- *Choice of friends:* Choose your friends wisely, friends who are positive influences and thinkers. They will help position you to unleash your potential.
- *Skill enhancement:* Find time to hone your skills. Read professional journals. Attend in-service training. Stay up-to-date.
- *Appreciation:* Be thankful for what you have been given. Show gratitude for the little things.

Finally, positioning yourself requires rest. God rested when He ended His work (Genesis 2:2). When the apostles returned to Jesus and told Him all that they had done, Jesus said to them, "Come ye yourselves apart into a desert place, and rest a while" (Mark 6:30–32).

Find time to rest in your bed (Isaiah 57:2–2). A sleep-deprived person is as dangerous as a drunk driver. You don't want to be caught sleeping on the job.

Make necessary *adjustments*

Adjustment requires sacrifice. We saw earlier in chapter 5 how the widow of Zarephath, who had planned her life, yielded to Elijah's request. She made a major adjustment, and she reaped in abundance. Adjustment is about giving up certain pleasures of the moment in order to achieve a goal, to attain greater heights. It is about giving of yourself.

Elisha had to make the adjustment (1 Kings 19:15–21). Elisha gave up all he had—his oxen, his farm, and his family—in order to attain elevation. He slaughtered all his animals and gave them to the community to eat. In other words, he didn't have any intention of going back to his former life. Even the great Syrian centurion submitted to him.

Moses's staff had been with him almost all his life. He was using it to keep his father-in-law's flock when God got his attention. God told him to drop it. Moses had to make the adjustment. He let go of his staff.

Then God asked him to pick it up again. When Moses picked up that same staff, it was no longer the staff of Moses; it had instantly transformed into the staff of God. We must be willing to let certain things go in order to position ourselves for success.

Jesus told Peter to cast his net again for a catch. Peter was an experienced fisherman, but when he decided to yield his knowledge, experience, and expertise to the command of Jesus, his life changed (Luke 5:1–10).

When God told Abraham to leave his hometown, God was asking Abraham to make an adjustment, to give up the comfort of his place of birth. Abraham obeyed, and he reaped the benefit of his obedience.

The rich young ruler, on the other hand, didn't want to adjust, and he left dejected.

Adjustment requires attitude change. When the angel of the Lord appeared, Gideon's view of himself was so low that he didn't think he was capable of accomplishing anything good. He had to adjust his thinking and his attitude, and that changed his perspective. When that happened, he became a mighty man of valor.

Don't say you can't. Remember that you can do all things through Christ, who gives you strength.

Adjustment requires determination. There are things we are used to doing. There are foods we are used to eating. There are friends we are used to keeping. But sometimes, in order to move forward, we must determine to make that required change. There will be challenges along the way, but we must be ready and willing to accept them, confront them, and move forward.

Deal with your fears

It was fear that kept the other eleven disciples in the boat. They were afraid of the storm, afraid of the unknown. Peter was afraid too, but he dealt with his fear. He confronted it head-on, and you know the rest of the story. Gideon was crippled by the fear of mediocrity. He was afraid of assuming responsibility, but he confronted his fear. Moses was afraid to face mighty Pharaoh, but he confronted his fear. There are countless examples of such people; you and I could be among them.

Fear can cause you to lose your chance of success. It intimidates you to a point where minor hills become mountains in your eyes. Ten spies went out to survey the Promised Land, but eight out of the ten were terrorized by fear (Numbers 13). They didn't believe that even God was able to help them. They concluded that it was impossible to take the land. Joshua and Caleb refused to be intimidated. They were ready to confront their fears, and they did. They encouraged the people of Israel to believe they were capable of possessing the land. They received their breakthrough. They were the only two from their generation to go into the Promised Land.

Everyone is afraid of something. It could be rejection or failure; it could be heights or even animals. My wife is afraid of dogs and will not visit anyone who has a dog in the house. It doesn't matter if you are her patient. You must first put the dog away in a cage outside.

I am afraid of snakes. If I see a snake near my house, I will not return until the snake has been killed (by someone else), and I can see that it is dead.

The fears that engross us throughout our daily lives are unlimited. These fears can hold us back from enjoying our gifts, from putting a foot forward, from unleashing our potential. Having the courage to work through our fears can bring empowerment, a sense of accomplishment, and the readiness to take that STEP!

Being afraid doesn't necessarily mean we are incapable; it just means that we are not ready to overcome that fear yet. Having a great support system to encourage us to trample our fears can be a huge blessing in our times of need.

A friend of mine worked as a geologist with an oil company. He was a very hardworking man, dedicated and skillful. A supervisory position became available, and he was offered the position. Part of the requirements for the new job involved diving into the ocean. But he was afraid of deep water, and "deep water" for him was any level above his knee.

When he realized that he would have to dive in the ocean, he became mortified with fear. He called his regional manager and told him that he didn't want the position. He would rather keep his current position than risk his life jumping into the ocean.

All through that period, my friend would not eat. He would not smile. Everyone knew that something was wrong.

His wife encouraged him to take swimming lessons. This was a man in his middle fifties. He listened. He made the decision to confront his fear. He took swimming lessons all through the summer. It was a challenge, but he got through it. And he got the job! Thank God for a supportive wife. Thank God for a patient regional manager.

When I was in primary school, we were required to memorize the multiplication table on the back of our exercise book. Every morning, the teacher would have us recite it. It was the worst experience of my life, especially when the teacher called me out to recite it in front of everybody. Perhaps he had heard me mumbling and fumbling. I resented mathematics so much that I didn't want to have anything to do with it.

I managed to go on without getting too involved with math. Then, when I got to high school, we had a young teacher who did nothing but show off his mathematical magic on the chalkboard. One day, he wrote:

dy dx = 0
d is the distance
y is the number of yards
x is unknown

Do you know that even today, *x* remains unknown? Fear gripped me: fear of mathematics, fear of the unknown.

The huge challenge for me was that to pass the West African School Certificate exam, one must pass mathematics. My problem had begun. Would I decide to confront mathematics, or would I end up a poor village farmer?

I made a decision to confront this giant on my way to unleash. There was a senior student who was nicknamed "Chico Obi" because of his excellent math skills. Chico Obi was a renowned mathematician in Nigeria. Anyone who exhibited mathematical skills was referred to as Chico Obi. I went to him and told him my dilemma. He was kind enough to spend time with me, and I was able to pass mathematics. I still don't like math now, but I didn't allow it to stop me.

My daughter's best friend had always been afraid of heights, to the extent that she refused to travel by air or stay above the fourth floor of a high-rise hotel. Standing on high ground was torture. Until she realized that she was stronger than her fear, she allowed that fear to diminish her sense of self-confidence.

The first time she acknowledged that she was afraid of heights was when her family went on a vacation. She was about six years old then. They went to San Antonio River Walk and stayed at the beautiful Marriot River Walk hotel. The hotel had a mall on one side and the River Walk was on the other, connected by an open walkway over the water. As the family walked up the stairs and started across, my daughter's friend suddenly froze. She realized how high above the ground she was. Her father immediately ran up to her and put her on his shoulders, and she held his head tightly.

She confessed later that for many years after the River Walk experience, just the idea of being up high had given her chills. Whenever she found herself looking down from a high place, she could feel her heart beat a thousand times in a second. Her teeth would chatter like china dishes on a buckboard, and her knees would quiver.

She recalled an occasion when she went with her siblings to Fiesta, Texas. She walked up the stairs to the roller coaster because she wanted so badly to experience the thrill of the ride. At some point she looked down, and she felt something freeze inside her. She was so petrified that she had to squat down with her eyes closed. Her older sister had to leave a position in line to come to her rescue. Her sister held her tightly and helped her down the steps. That experience never left her, she said. She felt woozy at even the thought of looking down from a high level.

She made the decision to face her fears. She promised her siblings that she would not let them down the next time around. She enrolled in the YMCA to participate in activities that dealt with overcoming the fear of heights.

Part of the exercise was to run up and down a steep slope, which got higher and higher as you proceeded, and then walk over a high bridge across a bayou by holding on to a rope. The first thing she did was follow the lead of her friends who had done this in the past. When she reached the middle of the bridge, she looked down, and she saw the water below. She confessed that trusting a rope to hold her through that ordeal was a terrifying experience. She felt that panic creeping in. The temptation was there to just give up. Her stomach somersaulted like a porpoise in deep water.

Then she felt her feet wobble. She panicked, but she kept saying to herself, "I've got to do this! I've got to do this!" She said it with lots of prayers. Below the narrow bridge was a safety net, but no one fell off, including her! She was very glad she had been able to do it, and she began to gain confidence in her ability to overcome her fear.

Throughout that summer and beyond, she worked herself gradually through other heights. She rode the elevators of her dad's office building to the fifteenth floor and looked down from the window. Then she went with her sisters to Schlitterbahn Water Park. She was able to climb up the wooden stairs to the top. She didn't freeze. Her knees didn't knock as much. Her heart raced, but just a little. Her teeth didn't chatter. She was able to experience a roller coaster ride for the first time.

When she got off the ride, she had no doubt in her mind that something had happened to her. She had overcome her fear of heights simply because she had done something about it. She acknowledged the fear and then faced it squarely, believing that she was ready to move past it. She was proud of herself. She then began to pursue a career as an air hostess, something she had always had passion for, admired, and dreamed of becoming.

Pastor Joel Osteen dealt with his fears. Gideon dealt with his fears. Moses dealt with his fears. Peter dealt with his fears. My daughter's friend dealt with her fears. Don't let your fear stop you. Don't let fear rob you of your dream. Identify your fear, if you haven't already done so. Then confront it, and you will be free to unleash your potential.

Locate your opportunity

Sometimes our opportunities are there, but we don't see them. We wait for the opportunities to come to us rather than seeking out the opportunities. Zacchaeus the tax collector went out to locate his opportunity. He didn't just sit in his tax office. He was a short man, and he had to climb a tree to locate his opportunity. He did it. In fact, because he was determined to seek out his opportunity, his opportunity sought him out in turn. Jesus saw him up in the tree and invited him to come down.

When the woman with the issue of blood heard that Jesus was in town, she didn't stay at home and send someone to bring Jesus to her. She was very sick and weak, but she still got up and went seeking her opportunity. She did it, and she was made whole.

Moses could have just ignored the burning bush. After all, he had no business with it. But something caught his attention; there was fire, but the leaves were not scorched. He went to find out what was going on. It was there he met his opportunity.

Blind Bartimaeus had a good excuse not to get up and go—he was blind. But he heard a noise, and he immediately put in his inquiry. He was told that Jesus of Nazareth was passing by. He couldn't tell which direction his opportunity was coming from or going to, but he sensed that his breakthrough was here. He began to shout and scream. Then his opportunity heard him, and his life changed.

Peter saw Jesus walking on water. Peter didn't sit there waiting for Jesus to come into the boat. Peter went out boldly to locate his opportunity. If Peter had stayed in the comfort of the boat, waiting for Jesus to come, Jesus would have met him in the boat. Then Peter wouldn't have walked on water, and that opportunity would have eluded him.

We have to be doing something—something meaningful. It may not be lucrative, but it must be productive. Idle hands and minds don't get promoted. Moses was tending Jethro's sheep when God called him (Exodus 3:1–4). Elisha was on his farm when Elijah found him (1 Kings 19:19). Gideon was threshing wheat in a winepress when the angel of the Lord called him (Judges 6:11–12). When Jesus called the sons of Zebedee, they were at work (Matthew 4:18–19). Matthew, the tax collector, was at work when Jesus called him (Matthew 9:9). If you think you are too short, climb a tree. If you can't see, use your voice.

If you are a high school student, search the Web for scholarships. If you don't have a job, get up and seek out the openings. If you need a career change, get up and find it! If you seek to further your education, apply for admission and enroll in those courses. Arise, take up your bed, and walk. Take that STEP!

Be *optimistic*

It is difficult to remain positive when everything around you is negative. Life can be a roller coaster ride, a jogging trail with undulating topography. You must hold your head up and know that any rough situation you are facing will pass. There is always light, as they say, at the end of the tunnel.

I cannot tell you how long the lame man at the Beautiful gate had sat there begging for money, but somehow he knew that help was on the way. I cannot tell you how long the homeless man who found an expensive engagement ring in his cup had been out there begging for money, but he knew that one day his time to shine would come. I cannot tell you how many doctors the woman with the issue of blood had consulted, but somehow, she knew when her healing was on the way. I cannot tell you how long blind Bartimaeus had been without sight, but somehow he knew that he would one day be able to see.

My prayer is that God will open our eyes of understanding to see that they who are with us are greater than they who are against us. We must be able to look past our present circumstances and declare that it is well with us. When you fall, rise; when you fail, adjust. It is our ability to cope with our frustrations and setbacks that helps our optimism. Optimism inspires hope and enables us to work harder. We cannot just say that all will be well without making personal effort to get better.

Cultivate your gift

We all have gifts, but most of our gifts are left undeveloped or underdeveloped. Our gifts are embedded in the recesses of our very being, in our BACKPACK, and we must stir them up. We must nourish them in order to bring them to life. It is from these that we find creativity, love, and joy. Our motivation to utilize our gifts goes beyond the paycheck; our motivation is intrinsic.

A little boy told his father that his friends had different kinds of trees in their compounds, including guava, mango, and orange. He asked his father if he could plant such trees in their own compound. His father granted the request and gave the little boy a mango seed to start. Every day, this little boy kept his eye on the spot where he had planted the mango seed. Day after day, he sat and watched, but nothing was happening. The seed was not germinating.

One day, his father came home and saw him weeping. His father asked him why he was weeping. The little boy told his father his sad story.

"When was the last time you watered the ground?" his father asked.

"I haven't," responded the boy.

"Don't just watch it; water it!" his father said.

The little boy watered the ground and spent time pulling the weeds, and soon a mango tendril appeared.

The same applies to our gifts. We have to till the ground and spend time nurturing our gifts. We cannot expect to reap bountifully if we have not worked hard. You can cultivate your gift by attending conferences, joining an association, reading books and journals, or working alongside someone with similar giftedness. Elisha worked with Elijah, and his gift came alive.

Keep an open mind

Some of us like to sit in the same pew every Sunday and talk with the same people all the time. We like to eat the same food and don't want to try something new.

It is always a good idea to keep our minds open. This applies not only to food, but to our associations with people, regardless of age, gender, culture, ethnicity, and linguistic background. We must learn to appreciate people and listen to other ideas. This opens up a world of opportunities and possibilities that we would never otherwise imagine.

When Abraham, then Abram, left his father's land, he also took his nephew, Lot, with him (Genesis 13). When the land could no longer support both of them because their possessions were so great and disputes arose, Abram had to make a decision. To avoid quarrels within the family and to pursue peace, Abram humbly told Lot to choose the area of land he would like to possess.

Abram was an open-minded person. Lot was his nephew, a child to Abram, but Abram yielded to him. Some of us in a similar situation might say things like, "I brought you to this place, and I can ship you back home," or "I brought you into this world, and I can take you out."

Notice that as soon as Lot chose, God said to Abram, "Look around from where you are, to the north and south, to the east and west. All the land that you see I will give to you and your offspring forever" (Genesis 13:14–15).

Keeping an open mind involves being truthful, especially to yourself. There should be no pretense. No one wakes up in the morning and decides to have an open mind for that day. You must make it a part of your everyday life.

12

It Takes a Process

An African proverb says, "If you told a poor man what it would take to become rich, he probably would prefer to remain poor." Nothing great comes easy. Success is a process.

Booker T. Washington once defined success as a measure not of the position one has attained in life but of the obstacles one has overcome while trying to succeed. Success requires determination, commitment, preparation, sacrifice, and exertion. In high school, we were made to memorize this quotation: "The height attained by successful men cannot be reached by a sudden flight, for they, while their companions slept, kept on burning their midnight lantern."

It is not the degree or diploma or certificate that one receives on the day of graduation that matters; it is the hard work, the struggle, the diligence, the resilience, the patience, and all the effort that went into achieving the degree that matter. You may not even need to be present on the day the diploma is awarded. It can be mailed to you. You can pick it up at a later date. You can even have someone pick it up for you. It is already earned!

A man came kneeling down before Jesus, asking Him to heal his son, who was "lunatic, and sore vexed: for oftentimes he falleth into fire, and oft into the water" (Matthew 17:15). The man had brought his son to the disciples, but they were not able to cure him. Part of Jesus's response was, "This kind goeth not out but by prayer and fasting" (Matthew 17:21).

The disciples had been with Jesus, so the man assumed that they could do what Jesus would do. He thought rightly. The disciples were capable, but they fell short because they had not tapped into the power of the anointing that was within them. Jesus's response showed that the unleashing of such potential takes fasting (courage, humility, and sacrifice) and prayer (dedication, patience, and faith).

In other words, before we put a foot forward, we must tap into our potential. We must continue to strive to reach our goal. That goal is not attained by sudden flight. It takes a process.

Joseph had his dream as a little boy, but he did not become governor until after many years. He had to go through trials and tribulations. Joseph put a foot forward. He knew that his brothers didn't like him; in fact, they hated him. He knew it, yet he agreed to take food to them in the wilderness. It was that single move that brought his dream to reality. When we put a foot forward, our caravan will come to take us to our Egypt.

David was anointed king in the presence of his brothers. He did not become king in Israel until twenty years later. He had to go through trials and tribulations.

Abraham was seventy-five years old when he was told that he would be the father of many nations. That did not come to pass until twenty-four years later. It took a process.

Remove fear, be patient, and allow God to take you through it, because He started it.

Isaac was born twenty-five years after God made the promise to Abraham. Jesus was twelve years old when He talked with the scribes and elders in the temple. We don't hear about Him again until He is thirty years old, eighteen years later. That was when He began to do what He came to the earth to do. Even while He was undertaking His ministry, He went through trials and tribulations.

When I was about eight years old, my father told me that I would go to America and become a doctor and a professor. That was a feat that could only be accomplished through fasting and prayer. It took a process.

My road to America was long, winding, narrow, and bumpy, with several detours. The Nigerian civil war had just ended, and its horrors still lingered: the physical ruin, the dilapidated homesteads, the desolate farmlands, and the horror of kwashiorkor-crippled children—hungry children with anguished, vacant eyes, shriveled chests, skeletal rib cages, distended bellies, and matchstick limbs. School buildings had collapsed. Everyone had been milked dry, both the rich and the poor.

I had passed the entrance examination into Methodist College Uzuakoli. Then high schools were called "colleges" in Nigeria. But school seemed to be the least of everyone's worries. My road to America appeared even more distant, almost unimaginable.

Uzuakoli town, where the high school was located, was very far away from Isuikwuato, my clan. I didn't have any relations living in Uzuakoli, and I knew no one I could live with, so becoming a day student was ruled out. But my father's words still rang loud and clear in my memory: "Onny, I want you to go to America and be like Dr. Zik Africa. You will go to America and become a doctor and a professor." Zik was the first president of the Federal Republic of Nigeria. Rumor had it that he studied in America and returned to become a great leader. I was determined to do something about this dream before it became a nightmare. I had to put a foot forward.

I took a job as a sharecropper. I worked on people's farmland, clearing the bushes and getting the ground ready for planting. I was contracted to till the fields and make mounds for the planting of yam and cassava. The unwritten contract always included breakfast and lunch on the farm and dinner at the home of the farm owner. Sometimes, I would work for the same person for a few days or weeks. Sometimes I would take a compulsory leave to nurse blisters on my palms.

I also hunted rabbits and sold them for money. One day, as I got off from work, I decided to dig into a hole that I suspected was a rabbit burrow. I had brought with me some dried palm fronds, matches, and a fan. I knelt down and began to dig. Intermittently, I lit up a dried frond and fanned the flame into the hole. The idea was to suffocate the rabbit inside and force it to run out. Occasionally I stopped and put my hand inside the hole to see if I could feel the rabbit's tail or fur or other indication that it was still there.

As I continued to dig, I saw something coming out of the hole, and it looked nothing like a rabbit. I stood up and ran backward, watching. A huge checkered snake was slithering its way out of the hole. I left all my tools and ran as fast as my tiny legs could carry me. I hated those monsters. My friends had told me that I ran from snakes not because I hated them, but because I was afraid of them. I didn't believe that. I just hated them! But my friends had the right to their own opinions.

I had boasted once of how I would crush a snake's head with my shoes if one dared come close to me. One day as I was visiting my friends, I saw a snake just by the gate to the compound. I let out a high-pitched scream that could have pierced deaf ears. As I stood frozen in fear, I heard my friends Chinyere and Chijioke giggling. They had hidden themselves in the bushes to watch what I would do. They had placed a tiny rubber snake by the gate in a strategic position. They were sure I would see it once I walked to the gate.

"Why didn't you crush that tiny snake with your shoes?" Chinyere asked, laughing.

"I thought you were not afraid of snakes," Chijioke added.

"Please call somebody to kill it," I pleaded.

"Kill what?" Chinyere asked.

"The snake! Didn't you see it?" I yelled.

"That was a rubber snake," Chijioke revealed, still laughing. "You could not even crush the head of a rubber snake."

That was ridiculous!

Anyway, on this rabbit-hunting venture, the snake was real, and I went straight home that day. On luckier days, a rabbit would emerge from the hole, and I would run it down, hit it to death with a stick, take it home, burn the fur off, cut it open, remove the bowels, pierce its skin with sticks, roast it in an open flame, and put it up for sale.

After working on people's farms and saving some money, I packed my suitcase and took a train to Uzuakoli. My big uncle's wife, Jane, had put together for me a small bag of *garri* (fried, dried granules of processed cassava root) and six heads of coconut. I was very grateful. I bought six cans of pasteurized (Peak) milk and a box of (Cabin) biscuits.

Those were enough provisions to last me for some time on campus. (Peak and Cabin were famous brand names students loved to purchase for their provisions.)

When I got to the school, I discovered that the semester was halfway over, and I had lost my place. I would have to wait another term to reapply. I was devastated. I had spent money I didn't have to get there, and would have to spend more to get home. I wept bitter tears and went back, helpless and hopeless.

Eventually, I saw this disappointment as an additional opportunity to work for more money. Perhaps I could afford to get an additional box of Cabin biscuits and a few more cans of Peak milk to augment my *garri* and coconut the next time around.

It was not long. The term ended, the next term began, and I was glad to return to Uzuakoli, this time for real.

Life at Methodist College Uzuakoli was fun and challenging. As soon as I walked into the school compound, I was greeted by the lush vegetation and undulating topography. The air was loaded with a pleasant scent of academic excellence. The students who had arrived earlier were already in their day outfits. Some had gone to the stream and were on their way back. Others were walking down the path in friendly groups, talking and laughing. The principal's house was right in front of the entrance gate, perhaps for a reason.

As I came closer to "the castle," the main students' hostel that included Carver, Hardy, William, and Aggrey houses, I noticed a group of boys standing under a tree. They were helping new students locate their assigned houses. One boy was nicknamed Ochongaloko, which means "troublemaker." The other was Ezo. They appeared very friendly. They came to me and helped me carry my luggage to my assigned dormitory, Hardy House.

The two boys and I later discovered that we were all from the same clan, Isuikwuato. Ochongaloko was from the village of Amaba, Ezo was from the village of Umuasua, and I was from the village of Otampa. We became good friends. Although Ezo was in class two then, he never treated Ochongaloko and me as "foxes," a term used to describe first-year students. They were considered wild, and their tails would have to be cut at some point to tame them. Ezo treated us like brothers.

I settled into my new environment. My experience as a boarding student at Uzuakoli was great. The school compound was beautiful. There were lots of trees, and the environment was fascinating. Class one students, in their attempt to show off their newly acquired vocabulary, would describe the school compound as "beautiful, with undulating topography." The school was in the middle of a village called Amamba. Village life filled the atmosphere with sounds of mortars pounding during the night, children running to the stream to fetch water during the day, and parents walking across the school to their farms.

There were two streams that students used. The villagers also used them. The students used water from one of the streams to wash their clothes, take baths, and the like. The other stream, called Azi, carried a special kind of water. It flowed directly from the rock and was clean and pure. That was the water students used for drinking.

To get to the Azi stream for pure water, one had to travel a distance and climb up and down a steep slope. The senior students would always demand that junior students fetch this water for them. When a school prefect punished a student for any offense, he would tell the student to fetch ten buckets of Azi water. One prefect was known for making students fill "Congo" buckets with Azi water. A Congo bucket was huge, almost the height of a normal first-year student. It was almost a sacrilege to use Azi water as bath water.

The path to the Azi stream was a historic one. It was the same road along which slaves were led away from Bende. It was the same road that Omenuko, the very first Igbo businessman, traveled with his apprentices. It evoked an aura of historicity. With such a rich historical backdrop, Methodist College Uzuakoli became for me, and perhaps all the boys, a landmark institution, an institution of the first class.

Azi water wasn't the only thing pure about the school. The students also strived for excellence in their everyday endeavors. In fact, it was a requirement in grammar and oratory that each person maintain excellence, such that students would guard themselves against making verbless sentences. Once in a while, a student would slip, and his verb would not match his noun. When that happened, everyone would seek cover to avoid being hit by a stray "bullet," a term used to describe the unleashed verbless sentence. Even school prefects sadly found themselves in such ugly situations, and when that happened, the other students would boo. There was a particular prefect who never made a sentence without error, and he was always quick to sentence any unlucky student he caught booing to "Azi water with Congo bucket."

Our senior prefect was smooth and eloquent. He would walk to the podium to begin his daily announcements flanked by two other prefects. He would begin by sweeping the assembly hall with his eyes, and then in a soft, calculated tone, he would deliver his speech with well-crafted punch lines. He would end by pronouncing punishment on students whose reports of misbehavior or disobedience had come to his attention. "Iheonunekwu," he would announce, "it came to my notice today that you ate your foo-foo with your fingers. You will therefore sweep the campus from the extension to the castle, and fetch a bucket of Azi water for every prefect. Is that clear?"

Of course, no other response was expected but a yes.

Fetching Azi water wasn't the only punishment given to students by school prefects. Cutting a field full of grass was another, especially at the beginning of a new term when the grass was overgrown. Mazi Uche was the best and only Igbo language teacher at the school. He was fond of assigning acres of overgrown field as punishment.

I had my own share of punishments. One day, one of the senior boys detained me under his bed for walking into his room without obtaining the proper permission. To be allowed into any dormitory, one had first to ask for permission. "May I come in?" I asked on this occasion, and then walked right in. The senior boy was upset because I hadn't waited for him to respond. I also hadn't asked properly. I had left off the word "please." The proper way to ask was, "May I please come in?" No one usually dared to go into a room until the senior student granted express permission to do so. So the senior boy detained me under his bed for bolting in.

As a result, before I could get to the chapel for morning assembly, they had begun to sing the college hymn; the doors had been closed. I was late. The prefect on duty would not entertain any excuses. So, I was punished again. This time, it wasn't under the bed. I was asked to cut a field, about half an acre of land with long blades of grass. By the time I was done, my palm was full of blisters.

Despite the intense discipline at Uzuakoli, I enjoyed being a student at Methodist College. A typical day began with early morning work. The prefect on duty rang the morning bell at about five thirty, triggering a stampede of students out of the dormitories. Some days, it was the rattle of the school chaplain's red Volkswagen Beetle that signaled the dawn of a new day. As the Beetle creaked to a stop, even the deaf, as the old saying went, would not need to be told that Agbagwu market was in session.

Every student knew what his assignment was. Some swept the paths, some worked on the flower beds, some drew water from the stream, some got the dining hall ready for breakfast, and others performed sundry assignments.

Then every student took a bath and got dressed for school, and the bell rang for breakfast. Food was served in an open, half-walled area in the middle of the castle. Students lined the four corners of the dining room, waiting for the dining hall prefect to declare breakfast ready. Some whose friends served on the food committee might ask for *adikwo* (additional quantity). Tables were set according to houses. Students from Hardy House sat together, students from Williams House sat together, and so on. Grace was sung and breakfast began.

After breakfast, we retired to our dormitories to get ready to go to the chapel for morning devotion. Soon, the big bell rang. The big bell had a home in the ceiling of the main assembly hall. Only the strong rang that bell. It was huge, with a long rope hanging from it. When it rang, everyone in the neighboring village could hear it. It was that loud.

My good friend Chris was the bell ringer, and he was strong. Chris was also from Isuikwuato. His father and my father were very close friends.

After the bell had been rung, all the prefects hung around, waiting for latecomers. No one walked; everyone ran or pretended to run, especially when a prefect was watching.

Prayer, praise, and worship in the chapel and singing of the college hymn were always part of the devotion. I loved to sing the college hymn. At the end of every assembly, everyone would stand and sing:

> Praise to the Lord, the Almighty, the King of creation.
> O my soul, praise Him, for He is thy shield and salvation.
> All he who hear,
> Brothers and sisters draw near.
> Praise Him with glad adoration.

All announcements for the day were made during morning devotion. House prefects announced the names of those who had committed one offence or another, and punishment was meted out. Punishments at Uzuakoli spanned from simple kneeling down to expulsion. The prefects had the power to impose most punishments, but not the power to expel students. The principal was the only one who could expel a student. Although expulsion was rare, there were a few times when one or two students got that ultimate punishment.

On a day when such announcement would be made, one could feel the tension among the students in the hall. I recall when one of my friends, Obele, was sent home. He had been caught jumping over a locked fence after hours to go to Amamba village. I really couldn't tell what his motive was, but he took the chance. Students had been warned not to leave campus after hours. Unfortunately for him, the school chaplain was driving by that night. Obele tried to escape, but it was too late. The car's headlights were so bright that the chaplain recognized him instantly.

So when the huge ceiling bell rang on that fateful afternoon, interrupting classes, everyone knew immediately, as the saying went, that a frog did not run in the daytime for nothing; it was either chasing after something or something was chasing it. The ceiling bell did not ordinarily ring in the middle of classes. It would ring for dismissal.

Soon the chapel was packed with breathless students. The principal walked briskly up to the podium, pulling his pants up almost above his belly button.

"Where is Obele?" he asked, adjusting the spectacles on his nose.

"Here, sir," Obele said, standing quietly.

"*Nwa m, I ga-ala* (My son, you must go home)," the principal said calmly.

Obele, with his face turned down, knew he was in for big trouble. He would have to figure out what to tell his parents. The semester was only halfway over.

Immediately, Obele's house prefect escorted him to his dormitory, where he packed his belongings and left. That was it for Obele and Uzuakoli. He enrolled in another school somewhere in Aba.

That was the Methodist College Uzuakoli that I attended.

The education we received was extremely competitive, both in sports and academics. In academics, everybody wanted to beat everybody, but at the end of it all, one person would always emerge as the top student. Most of the time, half a point would separate the number one student from the number two student.

At the end of the school day, every student retired for lunch, followed by an afternoon siesta. Then the bell rang again, and everyone went to the classrooms for prep, followed by free time in the evening for sports and recreation. The day ended after dinner with each of the houses conducting its own evening worship.

I was a member of the school choir. Reverend Rogers was our choirmaster. He taught us many songs. My favorite was a marching song that spoke about the promises of God.

My favorite sport was soccer. I played for my house, Hardy House, during interhouse soccer competition. My nickname was Skipper Olololo, and I had a friend, teammate, and roommate nicknamed Surpriser. He was nice looking and full of surprises, especially on the soccer field; he would always exhibit a new body movement or new footwork.

The junior soccer team traveled to different schools for soccer tournaments. It was a fun and exciting time for me. There was a particular song that we sang before every soccer match, and I loved that song very much. It inspired and motivated me to do well for my school.

Upon the soccer field
Before the game begins
We seek, O Lord, your sheltering shield
And surely we must win …
Up Uzumeco!

We were taught how to dress properly. There were three types of uniforms: one to attend classes (khaki shorts, white shirt, white tennis shoes and white socks, or sandals), one to go to church on Sundays (white shorts, white shirt, white tennis shoes and white socks), and a day outfit (red-striped shirt and khaki shorts). No one dared put on street clothes, or what they called mufti, at any time, and the clothes had to be clean and ironed. The day outfit could be worn on visiting days or for outings on Agbagwu market days.

We were taught how to use forks and knives and other proper dining etiquette. Prefects would roam all over the dining hall looking for anyone who dared to make a sound while eating. All one heard was the clanking of spoons, forks, and knives. The prefects were powerful. They trashed the food of anyone found eating with his fingers. Additional punishment could be meted out, depending on the mood of the prefect who caught him or the demeanor of the person who was caught.

Every meal began with grace. Sometimes we sang the grace; other times the prefect on duty said a short prayer or appointed someone to do so. Some nice prefects knew the students were hungry and said a short prayer or sang a short grace. The short prayer was really short: "For the food before us, we thank thee, O Lord, Amen!" And everyone would respond, "Amen."

Other prefects asked for a long grace regardless of how hungry we were. The long grace was really long and sung to the tune of "And can it be that I should gain an interest in my Savior's blood."

> We thank thee Lord, for this our food;
> We praise thee more for Jesus's blood;
> Let manner to our souls be given;
> The bread of life sent down from heaven.

I loved to lead the grace. My favorite short graces were "Ten Thousand Times," "Some People Have Their Food," and "Break Thou the Bread of Life." I led, and the others followed.

I joined the dramatic society. I loved acting, and I played many major roles in the plays. I was the town crier in *The King's Daughter*. I was the old man Okorie in *Jewels of the Shrine*, which also starred my good friend, Ogbo, as the Stranger and Grant as Okorie's daughter. My favorite role was Bambulu in *This Is Our Chance*, especially because of the big words I dazzled my audience with.

At the end of my first year, after the final exam, something remarkable happened. As I walked outside the classroom, I saw a group of class two students standing with buckets of water, rotten bananas, and leftover plates of food in their hands. It turned out that they were waiting for us, the class one students, to come out. Some of them were my friends. Eze, who was nicknamed Orpheus the Singer, seemed to be the leader. His nickname derived from his skill in playing the harmonica.

"Hey, Nwa Anu (fox), hop down here!" Orpheus commanded.

I looked at him, wondering whom he was referring to.

"I'm talking to you!" he screamed.

"Me?" I asked, beating my chest.

"Yes. You!" he replied.

I walked toward him, still carrying my stool and my books on my head. The other students went to take care of the other class one boys. They had us all kneeling down with our stools on our heads. I wondered why Orpheus of all people had chosen to humiliate me. I was his friend. We ate together and played together.

"Go back," he said, "and I mean hop down here."

Is he out of his mind? I thought. *He sees me carrying this stuff on my head, and he is asking me to hop toward him? Besides, I didn't do anything wrong to him.* I stood still for a while, wondering what to do next. I decided to ignore him and keep walking. That was a mistake.

The other class two students rushed toward me and pushed me down. My books littered the ground. I turned around and saw Ochongaloko dripping, water and rotten banana all over him. I then saw Ezo coming toward me with a bucket of water in his hand.

At first I thought Ezo was coming to rescue me, but he emptied the bucket of water over my head. I could not believe it. It was like Brutus and Caesar. "Even you, Ezo," I whispered and gave up every attempt to resist. Ezo shrieked with laughter and went away to "cut the tails" of the other foxes on campus.

"Who do you think you are?" Orpheus yelled at me. "You have the quack, the knack, the zeal, the impetus, even the audacity to disobey a second-year student. Kneel down there, you ugly fox!"

Orpheus was very much younger than me, and he and I were friends. I didn't understand how he could be so rude, disrespectful, and mean all of a sudden. I had just completed my final exams, and I was looking forward to going home. I looked at Orpheus with clenched teeth and a distasteful frown, muttering, "I will teach you a lesson later."

That was another mistake. He must have read my mind from my facial expression. "Pick up your stuff," he commanded.

I picked up my stuff that was littered all over the floor and put it into my bag.

"Walk on your knees with your books on your head," he said.

"Oh my God!" I muttered to myself. "You must be insane."

"Get up!" he yelled.

Well, I got up, thinking that the ordeal was over.

"Airplane turner." He and his friends began to sing:

Airplane turner
Turn, turn, turner
Airplane turner
Turn, turn, turner
Nwanu turner
Turn, turn, turner

I turned and turned and turned until I was dizzy. When they were done with me, they went looking for other first-year students. Ezo came to help me gather my things and clean up.

"It's the tradition here," Ezo explained, "a rite of passage, you know. Every fox must have his tail cut at the end of the first year. They did the same thing to us when we were first-year students."

I looked forward to the beginning of the next school year, when I would become a second-year student. I didn't think I would be that mean. I didn't think I would do that to someone whom I considered my friend. But guess what? I did.

I enjoyed Methodist College Uzuakoli. I made lots of friends. I went from being a compound chief to chapel prefect. I was also the leader of the school choir.

In my final year of school, I experienced a tremendous setback. A family emergency forced me to stay out of school for a whole term. There was no money for tuition, and I lost all hope of going back to school. The West African School Certificate Examination was coming up, and registration had started. You must be a final-year student to register for this exam. To be allowed to sit for the examination, one had to meet the registration deadline, and that was a far-fetched hope in my situation. My father was sick, and I didn't have money to pay the registration fees.

One day, my junior friend, Emmanuel, came to the village, looking for me. Every senior student was assigned a junior friend who helped him with activities of daily campus living, such as washing clothes, fetching water, making sure his plates were served with food in the cafeteria, and so on. This time, Emmanuel hadn't come to do any of that. His mission was different. He was a harbinger of good tidings. One of my classmates had registered me for the West African School Certification Examination, paid for it, and sent Emmanuel to my village to inform me.

That was how my dream suddenly came to life again. Without hesitation, I packed my bags and headed to Uzuakoli. Everyone was pleased to see me in school. After months of absence, I came back to discover that I was still the chapel prefect, my corner in the dormitory was still intact, and all my classmates were thrilled to have me. When the exam finally came and the results were out, I got one of the best results.

After our exam, my friends and I parted ways. On the final day, the principal preached and prayed, and he led us in the song "God be with you till we meet again." This was a powerful song. The principal spoke to us through the song. Each verse expressed his prayer for us all, and I appreciated it very much.

Most of my classmates went directly to the universities. Some joined the navy or air force. Some traveled to different parts of the country. Others traveled overseas to further their educations.

I had gained admission to the University of Nigeria, Nsukka, to study law, but I did not have the opportunity to go. Instead, I applied for the one-year universal primary education teacher training program, and I was granted admission into the teacher training college, Ihie Ngwa.

A year passed, and I earned my teacher certificate. After graduation, I was posted to teach at Nchara Oloko Primary School. Before long, I applied for and gained admission to the education program of Alvan Ikokwu College, after which I taught at a local high school in Mbawsi and then at Azuiyi Oloko on the outskirts of Umuahia town, about fifty kilometers away. This was all great experience, and I felt a deep passion for teaching. I loved the students, and they loved me. They fondly called me "Mazi." Mazi was a respectful title used to address an elder.

The people of this village also loved me very much, men and women, young and old. I was a young teacher and energetic. People had a great deal of respect for teachers and viewed them as the authorities in their classrooms. No one argued with teachers' decisions. Parents had their children fetch water for me and bring assorted fresh fruits and vegetables to me. I enjoyed all the attention. I fell in love with the place and thought I would remain there.

One day, a letter came to the school with my name on it. It bore the logo of the Institute of Management and Technology (IMT) on the envelope. I opened it, and the letter said I had been granted admission to study there.

That was an open door. I was not quite financially prepared to make the move, but I decided to put a foot forward, to unleash my potential. I had saved some money, and I knew that I could sustain myself for a semester or two.

I told the school principal of my plans. He was an Anglican minister. He told me that I could not experience the thrill of walking on water until I stepped out of the boat. I was encouraged, and I took the STEP. I seized the opportunity, took action by faith, encouraged myself in the Lord, and prayerfully followed God's lead.

Life on the IMT campus was different. Everybody minded his or her own business, pretty much. I was not able to get a hostel place because I arrived late, but I squatted with a friend, Kingsley, fondly known as Kenine, who was gracious enough to allow me to share his space. Kenine was a member of the campus soccer team, and that was why he was on the priority list for a hostel. Others on the priority list were those who came from out of state.

Before long, I had become acclimated to campus life. It was a fun, rich life, even for a poor student. Whole chicken was served on Sundays, with rice and stew. On Monday nights, fufu was served with bitter leaf soup and *okporoko* (stockfish). Oh, my goodness—you have no idea what luxury that was.

At one point, I seemed to have completely forgotten what I had come to IMT to do. We played draft in the evenings at the kiosk on campus. We roamed aimlessly from one hostel to the other in complete freedom. There were many activities to distract us, including campaigning for campus government offices.

I campaigned for one of my friends, Bona, who was running for the campus social coordinator. I carried a placard with his photo and slogan on it all around campus: "Bona for Social! Bona for Social!"

I sometimes hopped on a bus going from campus two to campus three. The bus was a medium-size type and carried only a few students at a time. That characteristic had earned it the nickname *oga abia ozo* (it will be back). Students who had classes on campus three and knew they were running late would gladly stand on the bus. Sometimes, students hung out of the door. It was hysterical. I felt very much at home and thought I would just stay there.

One afternoon, as I was walking to my room from the cafeteria, one of my friends ran up to me and told me that someone was looking for me. It happened to be one of my cousins. His parents resided in Enugu. At first, I thought something was wrong, but when I saw the smile on his face, I knew it wasn't something bad. In fact, he had been sent to bring some travel documents to me.

My sister, China, and her husband had asked me to send them some information. That had been long ago, and I had forgotten all about it. When I opened the envelope, I found an admission letter from the University of Houston, along with Form I-20 to support a student visa to the United States.

Excitement engrossed me, and I could not contain myself. That night, I could not sleep. I put the envelope on my bed and lay down on it. I didn't want any stories to be told about it. It was one of the longest nights I had ever experienced.

The next day, I began to make arrangements to travel to America, the land of my dreams.

My flight to America was scheduled to take off at midnight for an all-night flight to New York's JFK Airport. I spent several hours at Murtala Mohammed Airport in Lagos, having arrived eight hours too early. I was hungry, and I had no money to purchase anything. I had given my last cash to my favorite cousin, Esy, who was among the group that came to bid me farewell at Port-Harcourt Airport at Omagwa.

My stomach growled and pouted, squeezed and contracted. Leaning helplessly on a long bench by a window, my mind drifted in thoughts about where and how this road to America had begun. I couldn't tell if I was asleep or awake, but I recalled the events of the evening when my father gave me the ultimate promise. The series of events was vivid.

It was very late in the evening. The early morning rain that had shafted down the sky in a terrific cannonade of thunder had long ceased, and the clouds had dissipated, revealing the appearance of the moon in the distant skies. In the distance, I heard chants ring.

First there was a solo chant, perhaps from the one who first saw the moon; then another joined, then another, and another. Soon, the air was filled with a chorus of the old and the young, of men and women, singing and dancing in total jubilation for the beautiful appearance of the moon of harvest and plenty.

For some reason, I knew that evening would be very special. The appearance of the moon in the sky signaled the end of drought and scarcity and the beginning of harvest and plenty. I believed that the end had come for drought and scarcity in my life, and my season of harvest and plenty had begun.

The compounds had been cleaned; grounds had been swept. The noise of children running to the village stream to fetch water could be heard in the distance. The women had cleaned up the roadways, byways, and stream ways. The men had cleared the arena in preparation for the traditional dances and masquerade. Sounds of mortars could be heard pounding. The air was filled with smoke and the smell of burning goats and sheep hide. The aroma of stew filtered in intermittently, causing the tongue to salivate and the stomach to yearn for dinner.

Every child looked forward to this time of year. It was a time when family members came home from wherever they were, far and near. Train and bus stations were packed full with people waiting to welcome their folks. Even before the train could creak to a stop, family members called out names. Shouts of excitement rang as people found their relatives. Hawkers walked up and down the train tracks, shouting out their products for sale.

"Bread, sweet bread!"

"Water! Pure water!"

"*Ezigbo anu, onye choro ya!*" (Good meat for sale!)

But this particular evening was like no other evening. It was an especially different evening. Although it was the eve of the New Yam festival, it nursed a strong promise for me, an ultimate promise.

My father and I were in the barn, tidying the ropes and cleaning up. We had just finished staking the yams, strengthening the sticks and attaching palm branches and palm leaves to the fence to protect the yams from invasion by the goats. Apart from the rustling of dried palm fronds under our feet, the humming of the wind in my ears, the creaking of forest insects, and the singing of birds, all was quiet.

"Onny," my father called, breaking the silence.

"Yes, Papa?" I answered.

"I want you to go to school and be like Dr. Zik of Africa."

"Did you say school?" I asked, wide-eyed.

"Yes, son, I said school," Papa responded.

"And be like Zik?" I asked.

"Yes, son, like Zik," my father affirmed. "You will go to America and become a doctor and a professor."

I flung the palm leaves in my hand into the air, leaped with the elasticity of a cat, and dashed into the house. Niche, my older stepbrother, was sitting by the fireplace, playing his locally made xylophone.

"Niche! Do you know what Papa said?" I gasped.

"No," Niche replied.

"Papa said I would go to school!" I whispered in his ear.

"School?" Niche asked with muted excitement.

"Yes, Niche, school," I said.

"That's good. When did he tell you that?"

"Just now. Would you come too?"

"No," Niche responded. "You know, I don't want to go to school. I want to be a motor mechanic. But I am glad you are going to school."

"I am so glad," I said, "but I wish you could come too."

Niche began to walk toward his mother's house.

"Papa also said that I will go to America and become a doctor," I added.

"That's good, Onny. That's really good," Niche said, still walking.

Niche and I didn't get along very much. We were always fighting, even about very little things. One of my uncles, Dede Nta, thought that the best way to stop this mess was to give Niche and I a chance to just fight and beat each other up. He did. Dede Nta and Mama Ogo watched one day as Niche and I clawed on each other like Nchanga and Enoma, the characters in our primary five storybook that represented the sun and the moon in an eclipse. That was our last fight. From then on, we began to respect each other a little better.

Niche was not very much into school. He preferred to do other things. He always preached to me about how God made everyone different, and that his calling was not to go to school. His mother, Mama Ogo, did not seem to buy that idea. She did everything to convince Niche to go to school. At one point, he attempted school, but he did not like it. Mama Ogo would not give up on him. She went to any length to change what she called her son's silly attitude and stupid excuses.

One day, after perhaps consulting with some people, she came home and told Niche that he would be traveling with her to a neighboring village early the next morning. She had been told that the reason Niche did not like school was because of some *ogbanje* in him that needed to be taken out. *Ogbanje* is a wicked spirit that enters into a child, causing him to act strangely. The woman who had the power to remove it lived in the nearby village of Ozara. The medicine woman's name was Adanneochie.

She was powerful. Rumor had it that her power came from the river because she was the daughter of the river goddess, Nneochie.

Mama Ogo asked me to go with them so that my ogbanje could be taken out also. I had heard about this thing called ogbanje. It would kill a child prematurely. It would create obstacles in the way of progress. It would cause misfortune. I could understand why Mama Ogo thought Niche needed to go, perhaps to change his attitude toward school, but I didn't know why I had to go. I loved school, and I wasn't thinking about death and dying. Perhaps Mama Ogo knew something about me that I didn't know.

Very early the following morning, Mama Ogo, Niche, and I set off for the several miles' walk to the village of Ozara. It was still dark, and I was already scared and worried. Phantoms lurked here, there, and everywhere, as if they were coming to get me. I wanted to scream, but I held my peace.

We got there by midafternoon, and I was very hungry. We had been told not to eat before the visit. My stomach was growling. Niche appeared to be stronger. He showed signs of neither fear nor hunger. Perhaps he needed this more than I did.

We sat outside on a raised mud bench, waiting for the medicine woman to see us. Moments later, Adanneochie appeared from behind us. She was lean and short. Her head was bald, and she wore earrings made with tendril.

"You are all welcome," she greeted us.

"Thank you, Ma," Mama Ogo responded respectfully.

"I want you to know that I am expecting a visitor," Adanneochie added, "but do not be afraid or panic."

Neither Niche nor Mama Ogo nor I understood what she meant. I gazed at her with utter confusion and a troubled imagination.

Moments later, I saw the bushes wiggling and trembling. I sighted a huge, long monster slithering its way toward us. I jumped up and screamed, pointing toward the bushes. Niche saw what I saw and screamed. Mama Ogo held us close to her as she peered in that direction.

She too was beginning to panic, but she tried to calm us down as much as possible.

As the huge reptile made its way closer and closer to the house, Adanneochie reappeared and fed it with eggs. Then she asked it to go up on the roof. She called the snake Eke.

> *Eke, nyie elu.* (Python, climb up.)
> *Eke, nyie elu.*

The next thing we knew, the huge monster was on the roof. How it got up there, none of us could tell. We said nothing to each other. We just realized that we were in the presence of someone extraordinary. This truth intensified my fear, but most importantly, it boosted Mama Ogo's belief in Adanneochie's power to transform her son's life.

Adanneochie brought out a raffia mat, spread it on a mud bench on the veranda, sat down, and began to cut holes in Niche's palm. She showed Mama Ogo some dark, pebble-like things that came out of Niche's left palm. Niche screamed and cried tears of pain. He wriggled and twisted his neck in anguish. Blood was all over the floor. No one could rescue him, not even Mama Ogo. I cried with him, for him and for myself, knowing that I would be next.

When Adanneochie was done with Niche, I began to fidget. I would be next. My palm began to sweat. Drops cascaded from my head and face. I was getting myself ready when Mama Ogo announced that it was time to go home.

I was glad, but I wondered why Mama Ogo had brought me along. She later told me that Adanneochie had said that she and her people would visit me in my sleep and take my ogbanje out. That was even more sinister and uncanny.

"Who are her people?" I asked.

"I don't know," Mama Ogo responded.

"Could Eke be among her people?" I inquired.

"Onny, I told you I don't know," Mama Ogo whispered impatiently through clenched teeth.

On our way home, I thought about Eke the python and Adanneochie. I thought about the moment Eke appeared from the bushes. The more I thought about these things, the drier my lips became.

Niche held his left wrist with his scorched palm facing up. The medicine woman had squeezed some sap from medicinal herbs onto the cuts. Niche didn't say a word all through the journey home.

We got home late that evening. That night, I was very afraid, to say the least. I didn't know when Adanneochie and her entourage would come or in what form they would come. My fear became intensified by the thought of a story that was told about Adanneochie, the medicine woman.

Her father, Chief Omenuju, had married a river goddess, Nneochie, who bore him a child named Adanneochie, who later became the medicine woman. The story was that Adanneochie's mother, after giving birth to her only child, ran back into the river from whence she had come and disappeared. It was also said that she continued to visit her daughter from time to time in different forms.

This horror was etched in my memory all evening. That night, every string I saw appeared to me like a snake. I struggled to stay awake, but I couldn't.

I woke up the next morning tired and worn, but there was no cut on my palm, and I couldn't recall seeing anybody in my sleep. No one asked me anything that morning—not Mama Ogo, not even Niche.

So, when I told Niche that I would be going to school and to America, Niche believed me. I also believed it because my father had said so.

I knew how poor we were. I knew how much my father struggled to provide for us every day. I had heard about people who were born with gold spoons in their mouths and those who were born with silver spoons. I began to deduce that there could be some who were born with plastic spoons and some with wooden spoons. Knowing, how poor my family was, I concluded that I must have been born with no spoon at all.

I had passed school age; my right hand could touch my left ear when placed over the top of my head (that was how school age was determined during my time). But I believed absolutely in my father, and I immediately embraced the dream of going to America.

Although America was a land very far away, my father's promise brought it closer to me, at least in my imagination. I would love to study there. I would love to become a professor.

I went to bed early that night. Usually on such moonlit nights, the boys would sit outside the *obi* (central house), waiting for dinner to be ready. They would listen to the men talk about bravery and manhood, about hunting and fishing expeditions, and about wars and conquests. The girls would help with the cooking, and the mothers would teach them what they needed to know to make their husbands happy.

But this particular night was different. The sun had crept behind the clouds and the moon had risen in its place. The flickering lamplight from the obi cast a quiet glow over the compound. It was a perfect night for storytelling, but my desire to get learning outweighed any interest in entertainment.

The night suddenly became longer. I woke up many times and peeked outside to see if the day had dawned. I opened one eye slowly; it was still dark outside. I squeezed both eyes tightly shut as if that would squeeze away the darkness.

The rooster crowed when the day had broken. I was excited. I quickly got ready and ran across to my father's obi. The door was half-open. The scent of a mosquito coil permeated the air. The rays of light pouring from the hurricane lamp sitting on a high window silhouetted the figure in the corner of the room. My father was offering his early morning ritual of prayers and thanksgiving, but today was a very special one. His son was going to school.

I tiptoed into the room. I didn't want to disturb the silence, which at that moment was sacred, a hymn to divinity, a prelude to holiness. The Divine Presence permeated the total being of my father that morning as he called on God Almighty on my behalf. I knelt beside him quietly and placed my head gently on his lap. At the conclusion of the prayers, we got up; he shook my hand, embraced me, and rubbed my hair vigorously, as if to awaken the brain to its responsibilities.

I was excited about my new slate and pencil, and especially about my school uniform of white shirt and brown khaki shorts. I was particularly excited about this rare opportunity to go to school, learn English, go to America, become a doctor, become a professor, and be like my hero, Dr. Zik.

I set off on the seven-mile walk to school with my wooden desk and stool balanced on my head. Dry leaves crunched beneath my footsteps as I trod barefoot down the bush path. My uncle, Mbayi, had fashioned my desk and stool. He was a local carpenter. He made coffins, wooden doors, windows, chairs, stools, and other pieces of furniture.

About half a mile from the school, I heard the school bell ring. It was eight o'clock, and I was late on my first day. I had been told about the teachers' *koboko*, a cane fashioned from tough animal leather. It was the major disciplinary tool for all types of offences. The popular adage at that time was "Save the whip and spoil the child." The last thing I wanted was to start my first day with lashes on my back and buttocks.

I had heard scary stories about the gate man, Mr. Archibong Ekpenyong. He was said to have his heart in the back of his chest. That was how mean and wicked he was. He was only a gate man, but he manhandled children, especially the latecomers. I didn't want to run into him at all. His knuckles were stiff and crooked, perhaps from so much whipping. He would curse sometimes in his native Ibibio dialect, especially when he did not want the children to understand, but they could tell it was bad. Children called him "Yam," because he had big calves, out of proportion with the rest of his legs.

Well, I secured my slate tightly under my left arm, held my desk and stool on my head with the other arm, and flung myself into the air like a Zen arrow flying through the forest. I ran like a well-lubricated paddlewheel, swift and sure. My thin legs cut the air in rapid, even strokes. The cool morning breeze sifted through my hair. Then I heard the school band playing. I knew I was definitely late.

"Hey! Come here." A short man with a thick moustache and scanty goatee was calling to me as I tried to sneak across the barbed-wire fence. It was the teacher we called "Mr. Wuru."

I snapped to attention like a marionette manipulated by some unseen hand. There were about ten others waiting to receive the koboko. I set my slate, desk, and stool down in the open field and sat among the other latecomers. My young mind dwelt on the many stories about teachers and their canes.

"*Wuru* (bend over)," the teacher said.

The boys executed the command, bending over and touching their toes with the tips of their fingers. Every one of them was shaking like a leaf brushed by a passing wind.

In fact, the teacher was a popular figure in the school and neighboring villages—a brusque, blustery man with a cheery disposition and an earthy, village-style sense of humor. He spoke a smattering of five languages, but handled only his tribal tongue with any degree of fluency.

He always wore colorful attire that echoed the varied tropical foliage that was a perennial backdrop to village life. Everyone called him Mr. Wuru. His real name was Kofi Kwame. His nickname was derived from his method of discipline: bend over!

Every teacher used the koboko, but not in the style of Mr. Wuru. Parents brought their recalcitrant and disobedient children to teachers for discipline. Children did not want to offend their parents to the point where they would be referred to Mr. Wuru. As a person, Mr. Wuru was a dove in the wind, but as a teacher, he was metal in the hurricane. At least, that was every student's thought.

So when I watched the other children receive Mr. Wuru's koboko, needless to say that my heart beat three hundred times in a split second. I trembled and unconsciously fingered a button that hung loosely from my shirt.

When it came my turn to receive the koboko, Mr. Wuru looked at me with a disapproving frown. I propped on my elbows with my chin in my hand and froze with fear.

"Wuru," the teacher said.

I bent over, and, like the clap of thunder, the whip cracked on my back and buttocks five times in quick succession. I let out a high-pitched scream that could pierce through a deaf ear. I rubbed my buttocks and sucked my breath in through my teeth. Tears came streaming down my cheeks. I could hear the other children from across the field, laughing and giggling. Their laughter joined a symphony of discordant noises that filled the morning air.

"Go over there," Mr. Wuru said, pointing to the open field.

I rubbed my buttocks vigorously and staggered to the field in front of the school building where all the teachers and pupils stood. It was the morning routine to inspect the children for cleanliness. My slate, desk, and stool were still in the open field. Since we came late, we were told to leave them there and to pick them up after the morning routine.

The school band was sitting at the corner of the field, dressed up in red khaki pants and long-sleeved white shirt. The band master signaled for the music to stop. Everyone was quiet, waiting expectantly.

"School, hands up!" shouted one of the teachers. He was the teacher on duty that morning.

All hands went up in the air.

"Down!"

"Up!"

"Down!"

"Up!"

"Clap one!"

All the children clapped above their heads.

"Clap two!"

"School, clap three!"

"Hands down!"

"Hands on your neighbor's shoulders—place!"

We executed the command, forming three straight lines with an arm's length of space between us.

"Hands down!"

"Right turn!"

"Hands in front—stretch!"

We stretched our hands out in front of us.

"INSPECTION!" he finally roared.

My fingernails were as long as a tiger's. I didn't know that I was supposed to cut them, especially on Mondays, the inspection days. No one had told me. Perhaps it was one of those things that one had to find out. I found out.

There was one teacher to a line. Mr. Wuru was assigned to inspect my line. I almost wet my shorts when I saw Mr. Wuru with his koboko.

The boy standing beside me had bushy hair, and the koboko descended on his head twice. His face broke into a distasteful, toothless grin.

I realized what was coming my way. I could almost hear my knees knocking in fear. My hair was neither cut nor combed, and my father had run his hands all over it earlier that morning. The koboko cracked the air, and the lash fell across my head and back.

"Next … time … cut … your … hair … bushman," Mr. Wuru said, flogging between each syllable. The whipping and his words seemed to synchronize.

"Yes, sir," I answered painfully, bouncing up and down like a ping-pong ball.

A boy standing beside me giggled.

"Shut up!" I snapped.

"Atten-tion!" the teacher on duty cried out. "By the left, mark time. Left, right, left, right. Forward march!"

The band began to play again. The teacher started a song, and everyone joined in. It was a familiar tune to me because I had heard schoolchildren sing it at home several times, so I joined in.

> I am H-A-P-P-Y
> I am H-A-P-P-Y
> I know
> I'm sure
> That I am H-A-P-P-Y.

The drums beat, and the flutes sang, and I marched on happily despite the beating I had received earlier. My excitement outweighed the pains I felt from the bruises I had sustained from the koboko.

To have the opportunity to go to school was an excitement in itself; not everyone had the opportunity. For me, it was the ultimate promise. The koboko was a part of going to school, and I knew it from the start.

So I stretched my hands as far as they could go—forward, backward, forward, backward, forward—alternately to the intoxicating, intricate rhythm of the village school band. Once in a while, my feet would lose the pace, and I would watch the other children's steps in order to fall back in rhythm. I even made up my own lyrics to go with the music.

I marched on and on, looking to my sides at intervals to see if anyone noticed how proud I was to be a pupil of St. Celina's Elementary School. Rivulets of hot, salty sweat streamed down my face and burned when a few of the droplets eased their way into the tiny cuts made by Mr. Wuru's koboko. I really didn't feel the hurt that much. I was happy to be in school.

One could see in my face the dawn of a new life as the other children and I stood in the school hall, listening to the headmaster welcome us to school. We sang some songs that morning. Most of them were new to me. I knew some of them. I had heard the other children sing them when they returned from school. When the students began to sing one of my favorites, I joined in:

> *O Dina, osisi mango*
> > *O Dina*
> *O Dina, osisi mango*
> > *O Dina*
> *I na-eri ji akpu?*
> > *Dina*
> *I na-eri alibo?*
> > *Dina*
> *I makwa kosi ato?*
> > *Dina*

We clapped and stamped and sang. Every child loved to sing. The songs, the singing, the clapping, and the dancing expressed different feelings—feelings of hope, joy, sorrow, grief, and loneliness.

Each day began with prayers. Above the assembly hall was a big round plaque on which was inscribed, "Cleanliness is next to godliness." The headmaster drew everyone's attention to it and told us that it was the school's motto. He read it aloud to us, and we all repeated after him.

"What's a motto?" I pondered. The headmaster must have read my mind; he explained to us what a motto was. I wondered if that was why we had to go through such a rigorous inspection every Monday morning.

Before we prayed, we sang songs from the *Songs of Praise* hymnal. They were all beautiful songs, but the one that stuck with me all day was "Pass me not, O gentle Savior." For some reason, I felt very secure and confident after the hymn.

While we closed our eyes to pray, I repeated my prayer from the previous night, and I was ready. Soon after, the assistant to the headmaster grouped the students in their classes. My teacher was Mr. Wuru.

Mr. Wuru appointed Bashuru to be the class monitor. Bashuru's main responsibilities included alerting the class of Mr. Wuru's entry, writing the names of noisemakers, arranging the teacher's desk, and carrying home his books, class register, and stool.

As the class monitor, Bashuru was allowed to use pen and ink. The pen was a wooden type with a nib. To write, one had to dip the nib into a bottle of ink.

Not everyone was allowed to write with pen and ink. It was a special privilege for those whose penmanship was exemplary. Some were stuck with a pencil for the entire year.

I was excited when Mr. Wuru cleared me to use pen and ink. My favorite ink color was blue. It looked beautiful on white paper. But Mr. Wuru insisted that all students use the blue-black ink. The first time I used ink, I was very proud. I even purposely smeared some on my white shirt, so that people who saw me would know that I was a scholar and that I had been approved to use pen and ink—not pencil. It was a proud feeling.

Mr. Wuru was fond of long words. People said he was a very learned man. His favorite hobby was copying jaw-breaking words from his *Chambers Etymological Dictionary* and baffling the children with them. Some of those words still echoed in my childhood memory: "tintinnabulation," "lackadaisical," "sonorous," "octogenarian," "cacophony," "auditory hallucination," "alacrity," and so on.

I learned some big words too and how to spell them. My first big word was "She-ke-le-ke-ban-go-shay." I learned how to spell it by syllable. I didn't know what that word meant. It was a popular word among the students, and I could spell it. That was all that mattered to him.

When Mr. Wuru walked into the classroom, Bashuru struck his stick three times on the desk. Everyone stood up.

"Good morning, sir!" everyone greeted the teacher in unison.

"Good morning, class. Please be seated," he said, walking to his desk.

It had always been that way. All the children had to sit still in their seats, ready to welcome the teacher. Everyone had to be quiet. The class monitor would write the name of anyone who dared to talk, and give it to Mr. Wuru.

When Mr. Wuru asked us to sit down, we all sat down at our desks, looking expectantly at the chalkboard. This ritual of greeting the teacher was done two times a day: once in the morning and once in the afternoon, after long recess.

Recess time was a fun time. It was time for free play. The students gathered in little groups to do their own things. Some played football, some ran races, and others just watched. I loved to do the *sanga* dance:

> *Sanga, Sanga*
> *E-hei*
> *Sanga, Sanga*
> *E-hei*
> *Sanga Bele Bele*
> *E-hei Belebe Sanga, E-hei!*

The dancers threw their legs forward and backward alternately to the rhythm. Then at "*Belebe Sanga,*" they would swirl around twice.

The girls played separately in their groups. They clapped and ran around the circle. Sometimes the boys would stop and watch them.

I was not really watching all of them. I had special interest in one girl. Her name was Okwere. Her father's house was near the village railway station and right behind the school.

Okwere was beautiful and slenderly built. She had dark eyes and a long neck. Her hair was always combed and dressed with multicolored beads.

Okwere didn't like me. Mr. Wuru had assigned her a desk close to mine, but she always moved her desk away. She refused to speak to me.

But at recess, my eyes were on her all through. I thought she was the best dancer in the group. One time, her eyes met mine, and I waved at her. She blushed and ran away. I wasn't too sure what she was thinking about at the time. I knew she didn't like me, but I liked her a lot.

On our way back to the classroom, I felt a slight pinch on my neck. I turned around and saw Okwere trying to hide behind one of her friends. Perhaps she liked me too, I thought.

After school that day, Okwere and I walked home together. We became good friends from then on. Some days, I would eat at her house before going home.

At the end of recess, everyone came in sweating. We used our books to fan off the heat. Some students used their clothes to wipe off the sweat.

The morning of my first day, as we sat down waiting silently, Mr. Wuru brought out a big, long, blue book with a hard cover. It was the class register. Everyone's name was supposed to be in it.

"My name is Mr. Kwame, and I am your teacher," Mr. Wuru announced, sitting on the edge of his table with his legs crossed. He took out a red pen from the side pocket of his shirt. There were about five pens of different colors clipped to that shirt pocket. He began to call the roll.

"Isiaka Abu."

"Present, sir."

"Vaku Abiodun."

"Present, sir."

"Aliku Ambrose."

"Present, sir."

He went on and on until he had called every name on his list, but my name was not in Mr. Wuru's roll book. Mr. Wuru asked me to see him after school. I was scared to death. I didn't know why my name was not on the list. I became very nervous.

"We will learn English today," Mr. Wuru said, spelling out the word "English" on the chalkboard.

I was glad. English was my ticket and gateway to America, and I was going to begin my learning with it.

"Repeat after me," said the teacher, pointing to a visual aid on the corner of the chalkboard.

Teacher:	A man.
Class:	A man.
Teacher:	A pan.
Class:	A pan.
Teacher:	A man and a pan.
Class:	A man and a pan.
Teacher:	A pan and a man.
Class:	A pan and a man.
Teacher:	He is a man.
Class:	He is a man.
Teacher:	It is a pan.
Class:	It is a pan.
Teacher:	(Pointing at a picture of a pan) Is this a man?
Class:	No, it is a pan.
Teacher:	(Pointing at a picture of a man) Is this a pan?
Class:	No, it is a man.
Teacher:	Very good! Now, listen very carefully. I am standing up. What am I doing?
Class:	I am standing up.
Teacher:	No! No! No! Your response should be, "*You* are standing up." Now, what am I doing?
Class:	You are standing up.
Teacher:	Again.
Class:	You are standing up.
Teacher:	Again.
Class:	You are standing up.
Teacher:	Very, very good!

"What is your name?" Mr. Wuru asked, pointing at me.

"My name is Onny, sir," I answered.

"Good! Onny, stand up," Mr. Wuru said.

I slowly stood up. Learning English was all right, but not when I stood up for all eyes to watch me. As I stood, my mind seemed to have sat down, and I began to shiver.

"What are you doing?" asked Mr. Wuru.

"You are standing up," I responded faintly.

"What are you, you doing?" Mr. Wuru asked again, pointing at me.

"You are standing up," I responded, gulping in my words like beads of dark water.

"No! No! No! No! No!" yelled Mr. Wuru impatiently. "What are you, I mean *you*, doing?"

I stood very confused. My fingers fidgeted at the sides of my brown khaki shorts. I looked down to my right, listening for a whisper from Ogele, a boy sitting next to me. Ogele did not dare to make a sound. Mr. Wuru was standing right there.

Hands were raised around me, and I felt more and more nervous, confused, and foolish. I could feel my stomach turn over, slowly, gradually, a porpoise in deep water, and I gave up any attempt to answer.

Mr. Wuru turned to the class and pointed at Bibiana, who was sitting beside me.

"Stand up," Mr. Wuru said. "What is your name?"

"My name is Bibiana Ogerinka, sir."

"Good, Bibiana. Tell me. What are you doing?"

"You are standing up," Bibiana answered.

"*Noooooooooooooooo!*" screamed Mr. Wuru, flinging his chalk through the window. A tense silence swept the room. One could hear a pin drop. Mr. Wuru paced from one end of the classroom to the other with his hands crossed behind his back.

A few moments later, he turned to Bibiana and quietly said, "Bibiana, my question is about you, not me. So, tell me, honey. What are you doing?"

"I don't know," Bibiana responded faintly.

"All right. Listen to me, girl. You are not sitting down. Are you? You are standing up. Aren't you? So tell me, what are you doing?" Mr. Wuru asked, gently and patiently.

"I am standing up," she replied.

"Good!" shouted Mr. Wuru. "Clap for her!"

The class clapped.

"Now, Onny, what is she doing?" Mr. Wuru asked, pointing at Bibiana.

"She is standing up!" I responded.

"Very good!" said Mr. Wuru. "Now, what am I doing?"

"I am standing up," I said, hoping that I had said it right that time. The class giggled. Mr. Wuru laughed cynically.

"I am standing up," Mr. Wuru repeated with his mouth twisted to one side of his face. "Look at your ugly mouth. I am standing up. Class, what am I doing?" One could tell from the tone of his voice that he was losing it.

"You are standing up," the class sang in chorus.

"Very, very good!" exclaimed Mr. Wuru with some relief. "Now, what is he doing?" he asked the class, pointing at me.

"You are standing up," they sang again in a loud chorus.

"No! No! No! No! No!" shouted Mr. Wuru, holding his head in his hands. "I am asking … What is he, he, I mean he, doing?" He pointed at me vigorously. His eyes bulged with anger.

The class was confused, nervous, and afraid. They quietly sang, "You are standing up."

"This is the worst class I've ever taught. Look here, you silly chicken heads. How long will it take you to understand simple things?" Mr. Wuru said, boiling with rage. "You all have a problem—a very big problem. All you know is how to eat *akpu*. Go home and practice it. You must say it correctly tomorrow. In fact, there will be no recess tomorrow until you get it right—every single one of you. Today, you may go for free play." Mr. Wuru left.

Angry at my poor performance, I now tried to reestablish myself by telling the other children what they ought to have answered: "He is standing up."

"Be quiet!" shouted Tobenna, whom we called Toby. "Why did you not say so when the teacher asked you, if you are that clever?"

Everybody in the school was afraid of Toby. He was very muscular and appeared older than everyone else in the class. He had flunked the class several times and was repeating it. His mother seemed to have gotten used to Toby not passing. Each time she was asked how Toby was doing in school, her response was always the same: "*O si n'elu nkwu da ozo o*! (He fell from a palm tree again)," meaning that Toby flunked his exam again.

Toby beat up people for nothing. When he pinned someone down, he wouldn't let go until the person called him "Dad" or "Uncle" or whatever else he wanted to be called. Everybody wanted to be his friend or tried to be on his good side. I didn't say a word as he barked at me.

His nickname was "Baddest." The name originated from his response to a question during a lesson on comparative and superlative degrees. The teacher had given him the word "bad" and asked him to state its comparative and superlative degrees. He had heard someone's response earlier on the word "fat"—"fat, fatter, fattest"—and so he responded, "Bad, badder, baddest."

The rest of the school day was great. We learned nature study and arithmetic. Before we left for the day, the teacher gave us a list of books to buy.

Not many parents could afford to send their children to school. Nothing was free, from primary school to college. One had to pay for everything—pencil, ruler, slate, chalk, books, and eraser, not to mention the almighty tuition.

I took my book list home, and my father brought me to the market to buy them. I really dreaded going to the market on rainy days. The markets were slippery and filthy with an atmosphere of breathless enterprise.

Throngs of people went in all directions, seeking the best bargains. Their scurry and hustle seemed overwhelmingly intensified by the cacophony of peddlers' voices shouting out their products: "Tango bread! Tango bread! One-one *naira*! *Oka, oka*! Ripe banana! *Akara*! *Akamu*! *Dodokido gbona re-o*! Hot moi-moi is here!"

The Agboro men transported heavy bags of *garri* and rice from one place to another on their backs. One dared not stand in their way. They would run a person over. Their energies seemed unleashed by the desire to make as many trips as they could before the day was over.

Many strange things happened in the market. Gamblers sat at different corners, trying to make a living through deceit. They lured folks in and tricked them into playing games that were rigged.

As my father and I entered the market, I watched as the gamblers cornered a young woman going to buy ingredients for soup for her family. The woman watched as the card player showed her the right card to pick in order to double her money.

He threw the cards on the mat, saying:

I were nke a, I rie m ego.
I were nke a, ego gi efuo.
E wekwala nke a, ma o bu nke a.
Akpakwala aka na nke a, ma o bu na nke a.
Nke a ka I ga-eji rie m ego.

If you take this one, you will win some money.
If you take this one, you will lose your money.
Don't take this one or this other one.
Don't touch this one or this other one.
This is the one that will win you money.

He showed the correct card to the woman and covered it up among other cards. For some reason, the right card seemed to have traded places with the wrong card. When she picked up what she thought was the right card, it turned out to be the wrong one.

They told her to try to win her money back by putting in some more money and playing again with just two cards instead of three. She picked a card up again, and it was the wrong one. She had lost all the money her husband had given her for food.

She grabbed the card player in desperation, begging to get her money back. The others in the gang pulled her away. Immediately, they took their mat and cards and disappeared, leaving the poor woman crying for help. She held her head with both hands pacing from one side of the market to another, shouting like a lunatic:

Chi m egbuo muo!
Ego afia di m nyelu m ka fa naalu muo!
A nwukwaanu muo!
Di m egbugokwa m taa o!

My God has killed me!
They took the money my husband gave me for the market!
I am dead!
My husband will kill me today!

Those who knew what had happened paid no attention to her. Those who didn't know the whole story tried to sympathize. They thought someone had stolen her money, but when they found out she had gambled, they had no more sympathy.

There is a story about a woman who needed to buy a wrapper, but she didn't have money to pay for it. She told the seller that she would like to bring in her friend to examine the wrapper to ascertain that it was worth the price. She went out and came back with a stranger, who examined the wrapper and confirmed its value.

The woman told the retailer that she would like to seek another opinion. So she asked the stranger she had brought in to wait there for a few minutes while she showed the wrapper to someone else. She left and never returned. She had used the stranger as her stooge while she stole the wrapper.

Market retailers grabbed the arms of customers and unleashed torrents of cajolery to bring them to their stalls. Some traders pulled the arms of young, beautiful girls, attempting to make passes at them. The girls cursed at them and would sometimes use a hand gesture of "*Waka, shege, banza ole,*" which means a useless thief.

But this rainy market day was different. I went with my father to buy my own schoolbooks. It was an overwhelming experience.

"Customer! Customer!" The traders called out to my father as we passed by their stalls. "Come and buy from me. I will give you a better price."

I watched as my father bargained with them. Sometimes my father walked away without buying anything, especially when the trader began bargaining from a very high price. At other times, he pretended to leave, forcing the trader to reduce the price for fear of losing the sale. Sometimes the traders were defiant and allowed us to go. Some of them appeared hurt or insulted by a low offer. Some didn't even dignify my father's low offer with a response.

My father ended up buying some of the required textbooks and materials, but he left some out. He told me that he would buy the rest another time. He also told me that he would go to the school to pay my school fees. I was happy.

There were times when my father could not come up with the school fees, and I was asked to go home until I brought my money. There were many others who shared the same difficulty. Sometimes a crack of the whip across our backs would herald our departure, as if it were our fault that our parents couldn't afford to pay the fees on time.

There were some lucky children who were never sent home. Their parents didn't have any difficulty paying their school fees. Isiaka was one of them. His parents were rich. They had a driver drop Isiaka off at school every morning and pick him up after school. His uniform was always clean and ironed.

Everyone wanted to be Isiaka's friend because he always brought money to school to buy *akara* (bean cake made with ground beans, pepper, onions, and salt, mixed with water, and fried in vegetable oil), roasted corn, and roasted groundnuts during recess. He seemed to enjoy the attention. He went around showing his money to his friends.

But Isiaka had a problem. He could not add one plus one. His parents were willing to do anything to push him on, but nothing worked. Instead of using his actual name, Isiaka, some students teased him and called him Isi Aturu (sheep head), especially those who did not benefit from his generosity. Others called him Isi Aki (nut head), Isi Okuko (chicken head), or Itiboribo (dummy).

I was glad to be me. I was even thankful that I could go to school with the sons of the wealthy. When they sent us out of class to get our school fees, I would go home and run straight to the farm where my father was working. I would help him till the ground, cut the bushes, plant the seeds, or stake the yams.

Going to the farm with my father was fun. My father would not let me go every day, but when he did allow me to go, he made sure that I had my favorite farm food—roasted yam with red palm oil and fresh red and green pepper.

The yam was roasted in an open fire made with logs of wood. When the yam was done, my father would scrape off the burned surface with a knife and cut the vegetable into slices. He would then put some fresh red palm oil in a ceramic bowl, cut green and red pepper into tiny slices, and mix them with the red palm oil. My father and I would sit together under a shady tree and eat. Sometimes the yam was very hot, and we would have to keep our mouths open for a little while to let some of the heat out before we could chew.

After eating, we would rest for a while before going back to work. Most of the time after the food, I would do nothing else but run around on the farm, chasing one grasshopper after another. My favorite was the *igrube,* a giant grasshopper. Sometimes the chase led to an unpredictable adventure into the heart of the woods, away from the sounds of humanity. One could easily get lost in such an adventure. The igrube would fly and perch at very short intervals, enticing its predator.

I got lost several times, and my father would call out. I followed his big voice back to where he was. I would then gather firewood and tie it up in bundles for sale.

I couldn't continue with school because my father got sick. There was no one to help me with the cost of school materials and tuition. I went to my uncle's house at Emene to seek help, but he turned me away. I also went to Abakaliki to one of my cousins who resided and worked there, but he gave me no help. I went home hurting and crying.

I missed many months of school. I sat beside my father's sickbed and prayed to God not to let him die. God heard my prayers. My father recovered fully from that ill health, and I was able to go back to school.

I must have fallen asleep at some point on that long bench at the airport, or perhaps I was in a trance. Whatever it was, it was vivid. I was on an airplane bound for America. I heard the voice of the captain announce that the aircraft would be touching down shortly.

Suddenly, I could no longer hear a thing. My ears were blocked. It got so painful that I could no longer bear it. I struggled to scream, but I couldn't.

Then I felt a gentle nudge on my shoulder. I woke up. An elderly man in his late fifties was standing by me. I was startled.

"I am Alhaji Sani Ahmed. What is your name?" he asked.

"I am Onny," I responded faintly.

"Where are you going?" he asked.

"America."

"Have you been there before?"

"No; this is my first time," I answered.

"I'm going to New York," he said. "I am a businessman."

"Have you been there before?" I asked.

"Many times before," he said with a sense of accomplishment.

"I am a student. I am going to Houston—University of Houston," I added.

"Well, we will go together," he said, sitting down on the bench with me.

I was not sure why Alhaji came to me. I wasn't sure if I should have given him my information. We sat there for a minute in silence. Alhaji searched his briefcase for something that seemed very important to him. He took out a piece of paper and began to read it.

"This is my itinerary," he said, showing me the printed information on it.

I didn't think it was necessary for me to say anything, so I simply glanced at the piece of paper. I quietly felt my side pocket to make sure that my own paper was still there, and it was.

"Have you checked in?" he asked.

"Yes, sir," I replied.

"I would like you to do me a favor," Alhaji cleared his throat. "I have a lot of money with me, and it is not safe for me to carry it all with me. I would like you to hold some of it for me. When we get to New York, I'll take it from you."

He opened his briefcase and brought out bundles of money, American money. He handed them to me and helped me put them in my carry-on luggage. From then on, his eyes were all over me, watching my every movement. He followed me everywhere I went. He even followed me to the restroom. I knew Alhaji Ahmed wasn't interested in my well-being; he was just making sure that his money was safe.

It was a long flight to America, almost ten hours nonstop from Lagos's Murtala Mohammed Airport to New York's JFK. Finally, the Nigeria Airways captain announced that the aircraft would be touching down shortly. It was in the wee hours of the morning. I looked down from the window, and what I saw was far more fascinating than what I had imagined in my dreams. It was the most spectacular sight of my life. Different colored lights flickered below and created a dazzling, beautiful night scene. I was overcome by the beauty of the landscape, and I froze breathlessly before its magnificence.

The city flared like a beacon against the dark skies, watched by the silent stars. I didn't notice the flight attendant standing beside me. She nudged me a little as if to wake me up. She then handed me a piece of paper to fill out for immigration. I filled it out completely and gave it to her on my way out.

"Keep it," she said, handing it back to me. "You will need it."

I thanked her and left. As soon as I came out to the waiting area, Alhaji Ahmed whispered to me, "Let me have it now."

I opened my luggage and handed Alhaji his bundles. Alhaji gave me twenty dollars to keep. I was grateful, very grateful. We exchanged pleasantries and parted ways.

"Welcome to New York," one of the ladies at the gate greeted me. She must have been one of the airport workers. She had on a badge, but I didn't have the courage to look long enough to read the name on it.

"Is this your final stop, or are you in transit?" she inquired.

"This is not my final stop," I responded. "I am going to Houston."

"I like your accent," she said. "Where are you from?"

"From Nigeria," I responded.

"Have you been here before, or is this your first time?"

"This is my first time."

"Well, welcome to America," she said, putting out her hand for a handshake. "Do you know how to get to the baggage claim?"

"No," I replied.

"Go straight down and follow the signs," she said, pointing to the east end of the airport. "Once you get your luggage, ask for a taxi to take you to the domestic airport." She wrote the name of the airport down on a piece of paper and handed it to me. "It's called LaGuardia. Once again, welcome to America."

After several steps, I turned around to see if she was watching me, but she was gone. *How could she have been so nice to a stranger?* I thought.

Many thoughts raced through my mind. I thought about all the stories that were told about women in America. But this woman had been simply nice and helpful, very courteous and polite, even to someone she had just met for the first time.

It was extremely cold outside. Thin, wet snowflakes were drifting down from the sooty skies. A line of taxis stretched along the curb, waiting for passengers.

"Need a taxi?" one of the drivers asked.

"Yes," I responded.

He quickly popped up the trunk lid and loaded my luggage, as if he knew what I needed or where I was going. He opened the back door and ushered me in with a sweep of his hand.

"Where are you going?" the driver asked.

"I'm going to the local airport," I replied.

"I know, but where are you heading to?" he asked.

"I'm going to Houston." I replied.

"Where are you from?"

"I'm from Nigeria."

"I could tell from your accent," he said. "Have you been here before, or is this your first time?"

"This is my first time."

"You speak good English. Do y'all speak English in Africa?" he inquired.

"Yes," I responded, wondering why he did not already know that.

"That's interesting. Are you from Nigeria or Africa?"

"I am from Nigeria, and I am an African."

"Isn't Africa in Nigeria?" he asked.

"No, sir. Nigeria is in Africa. Africa is a continent just like North America, and Nigeria is in Africa just as New York is in the United States," I responded.

"You must be smart. Do y'all have schools over there in Nigeria?" he asked.

"What are you talking about?"

"I mean do y'all have schools in Africa?"

"Of course we do," I replied.

"That's interesting," said the man. "I heard that y'all live in huts and in trees and run around naked in the villages. Is that true?"

I ignored him this time, and there was silence for a short while. He noticed that I didn't want to dignify that question with a response. He thought rightly, because I was getting upset, but I didn't want to show it. I didn't know where he was going, and I wasn't sure where I would end up if I said anything ugly to him. I didn't understand how the taxi driver could be so ignorant and be so proud to exhibit it in public.

In less than thirty minutes, the taxi creaked to a stop. I was glad. The driver got out and helped me offload my luggage.

"Your fare is thirty bucks," he said.

"How much?" I asked.

"Thirty dollars," the driver replied.

"I only have twenty dollars," I said.

"What do you mean that's all you have? You can trade something in," the driver suggested.

"What do you mean by that?" I asked.

"You can give me something."

"I don't have anything to give you."

"You can make up the difference with your watch."

Another taxi driver standing nearby had been listening to the exchange. He walked up to us. "How much does he owe you?" he asked my driver.

"Ten dollars, brother," the driver replied.

"And you want his watch for ten dollars?" the other driver asked. "That's my homeboy. I'll give you ten bucks for him."

I thanked the Good Samaritan and asked him his name.

"My name is Ebere," he said, "but they call me Eby."

"You are my brother!" I exclaimed. "You speak like an American. Are you from Imo or Abia?"

"We are all the same, whether Imo or Abia," Eby responded. "Where are you going?"

"I'm going to Houston," I replied.

"With which airline?"

"I think it's Continental," I said, digging in my pocket for my itinerary. "Yes, it's Continental."

"You are at the right gate. Just go in there and check in. Have a safe trip to Houston," Eby said, extending his hand for a handshake.

It was daylight. The sun broke through a heavy overcast. The flight to Houston had just taken off. I had fallen asleep, and I couldn't tell how long the airplane had flown. The captain's announcement woke me up. I looked out the window, and my heart dropped.

"America the beautiful!" I exclaimed. There was something special about this country. Everything I had read about it in books was true, but the impact was truly of fresh impressions, untrammeled by prior knowledge. From up there, I could see a fertile land of high plateaus and lush green foliage. The vast land reached from the banks of a river to the dry plains and blue crater lakes that were tucked among the terraced hillsides. I watched with fascination as the airplane descended slowly, and I could see the land more closely.

Arriving in Houston, something struck me hard. As I was coming out of the baggage claim area through the automatic doors, a man walked up to me, mumbling something. His beard was unkempt. He wore a long black jacket over a weather-beaten brown pair of pants. His frazzled old boots dragged along the pavement.

"Can I get a dollar to buy me a sandwich?" he said pathetically.

"I don't have any money," I replied, too afraid to look at his face twice. I walked away, dragging my luggage to a different location. *Why is a person begging for money, hungry and wretched, in America?* I wondered. I was very confused and disappointed. Could I have come to the wrong country? The America of my dreams was different—a land of milk and honey, a land where darkness never falls, the Promised Land, the land of Canaan, God's heaven on earth.

Finding a job with my credentials from Nigeria was a test of endurance and patience. Having attended a teacher training college and other institutions of higher learning, and having taught for some years, I thought that in America I could continue my teaching career uninterrupted. When I turned in my transcript from the Nigerian teacher college for evaluation, I was told that my qualifications were the equivalent of an American high school diploma, and no one was allowed to teach in America without a bachelor's degree or the equivalent.

I gave them my other transcripts, hoping that would improve my chances of securing a good job, but those also didn't do anything for me. To teach, they advised, I would have to get a deficiency plan and get training from a recognized teachers' college in America.

Days were going by fast, and I needed money badly. I had given away all my money to my friends at the airport in my country. Now I wished I could have my money back with the snap of my fingers. After every attempt at getting a "decent" job failed, I decided to begin from zero.

I landed my first job at Taco Bell, a fast-food restaurant. My duties were to sweep and hose down the parking lot, empty the trash from the lobby, clean the tables, squeegee the glass windows and doors, clean the bathrooms, mop the floors, and other duties as assigned. I quickly discovered that "other duties" included offloading food and condiments from the huge delivery truck, stacking paper goods on the shelves, and storing the perishables in the walk-in cooler.

My first day on the job was quite an interesting experience. I arrived at work dressed in the uniform of brown pants, brown shirt, and brown cap given to me the previous evening, when I was hired. I didn't have a problem with uniforms. I had been used to wearing them almost all my life, even though my coworkers made fun of me and told me that I looked like a clown.

The store manager was also a foreigner, from Jordan. His name was Amed. He was nice to me and treated me with some kindness. When I arrived at seven o'clock that morning, Amed was already there. He opened the door and showed me where all my working tools were—long push broom, squeegee, bottle of glass cleaners, dust pan, toilet plunger, paper towels, and so on.

The parking lot was cluttered with paper, cups, plastic knives and folks, and all manner of discarded oddities. I was charged with making the entire place clean before the restaurant opened in the next hour. Sweeping the parking lot was not a new experience for me. In fact, it was something I had done as a child.

When I was a little boy, every morning my stepbrothers and I would take turns doing our morning chores. I would sweep the whole compound using the *aziza*, a long broom made from special tree stems bunched and tied together. I swept from one end of the compound to the other. Sometimes I even swept the road leading to the compound for good measure.

Every Saturday morning, the children of the village would gather at the *ama* (village square), and everyone was assigned a portion of the ama to sweep. If any child failed to show up for this weekly cleanup, that person would be liable for a fine. The fine was a small amount of money; however, if one refused to pay right away, whatever valuable item was in sight in the person's compound was confiscated until the fine was paid in full. Most of the time, live hens and goats were cornered, captured, and taken away.

Even as high school students at Methodist College Uzuakoli, sweeping the roads around the school compound and picking up litter along the way were among our daily morning routines. Each house had a portion of the school to sweep and keep clean. The house prefects assigned students streets to sweep. Sometimes the prefects would use these assignments as a form of punishment for recalcitrance and insubordination. I was in Hardy House, overlooking the slave road, and my house was responsible for keeping the slave road clean and tidy.

So sweeping the Taco Bell parking lot was not new to me. Although I was a grown man with a beard now, and old enough to have a family of my own, I still had fun doing it. I drew courage and inspiration from the things I had heard my father say: "Nothing good comes easy, son. You must persevere. Whatever you find yourself doing, do it with joy and a cheerful heart."

Moments later, an elderly cab driver drove up and stopped beside me.

"What time do you open?" he asked.

"I don't know. I am new," I replied.

"What part of Nigeria are you from?"

"How did you know that I am from Nigeria?" I asked.

"I can tell by looking at you."

Uh-oh, I thought.

"What's your name?" he asked.

"I'm Onny. And yours?"

"I'm Musagie, but they call me Sage."

"That's interesting," I said.

"So what part of Nigeria are you from?" Sage asked again.

"Abia State," I responded.

"Where in Abia State?"

"Why are you asking?"

"I'm also from Nigeria, from Bendel State. I came to United States ten years ago. My family is in Nigeria. I haven't been home since then. My children are grown now. I see them in the pictures they send to me. I miss them."

How could he have been here for ten years and still be driving a taxi? I wondered. "You couldn't find a job also?" I asked aloud.

"It's not that easy, my brother," Sage said, smiling. "Dem no go give you better job here. You have to do what you have to do to survive."

Sage told me how almost every foreigner who comes to America has to do one menial job or another, and how going to school was no longer a priority. One had to survive first before thinking about going to school. "I have a wife here also, an American," he added.

I looked at him with a disgusted frown. "How could you have a wife and children in Nigeria and have another wife here?"

"You no go understand, my brother," Sage said. "But you just come, so make you wait. You go see what I mean."

Sage must have read the disappointment on my face.

"Listen, my brother," he explained. "The reason I haven't gone home is because I don't have the documents to travel. If I go home now, that is it for me and America. I was a bank manager at home. Something happened, and I had to leave home to come to America. Things are tough here. I had to marry an American woman in order to get my papers so I can get a decent job, get some money, and travel home."

"You couldn't get a job in the bank?" I asked.

"Sooner or later, you will understand what I am saying. Take care," he said and drove off.

As I watched him drive away, I fell into a tempest of thought. I went home that day discouraged. Would I work at Taco Bell for ten years? Would my dream be wrapped up in a taco shell? What about my family and my friends at home? Would I ever see them again? How about going to school? How about—

I didn't want to complete that question. The thought of it devastated me.

Working at Taco Bell was an experience. I cleaned the parking lot for a long time. I picked up the empty cups and dirty taco and burrito wraps tossed all over. Sometimes I had to use gloves to pick up the leftovers run over by cars. Then I hosed down the whole lot to keep it looking clean. I took the trash heaped outside the back door to the Dumpster.

One day I gave a customer an ugly look when he tossed his burrito wrap and Pepsi cup out the window. The customer looked at me, smiled, and said, "I was just doing you a favor. You need a job, right? This will give you something to do."

I thought about it and concluded that the customer was absolutely right. I would not have a job if there were no mess in the parking lot.

I was beginning to get used to my new environment when I had another rude awakening. I was sick one day, and the shift manager offered to take me to a nearby clinic. I was shocked. This was a guy who didn't care about how I felt. He didn't want me to even sit down to take a break. He cursed me out most of the time and told me to go back to my home country. I was surprised that he would be so kind as to offer to take me to the clinic.

He assigned another employee to be in charge of the shift while he was gone. He called another employee to come in to cover my tasks. He drove to a shopping center and stopped. When I got out of the car, he pointed to a sign above the door and drove off laughing. It was a veterinary clinic.

I had read about ugly things that could happen in America, but this was one I hadn't thought could actually happen. It did. I walked back to the restaurant and sat down in the lobby in silence.

That day was the last time I saw that shift manager. He didn't return to work, and no one heard about him again.

Soon I got promoted. I was no longer out in the parking lot. I was assigned to work behind the front line. My new job description included making sure that the inside of the restaurant was clean, including the lobby area. I was also responsible for making sure that all the items needed for the front line were ready on demand.

My day began with frying tacos. I fried several pans of them, enough to last for the entire day and begin the next day. It was a sweaty, sticky job. The heat emanating from the frying oil was suffocating. I soon got used to it.

I peeled, washed, cut, and shredded lettuce, tomatoes, onions, and black olives. I shredded cheese with a Hobart machine. I swept and mopped the floors, squeegeed the glass doors and windows, and washed, rinsed, and sanitized the dishes.

My first car was a Datsun station wagon. The station wagon served a dual purpose: it was my residence and my ride to school. This "home" was always parked in the Taco Bell parking lot. Instead of driving to an apartment after school, I drove straight to the restaurant and parked my car. The worst days were the days when it rained and the humidity was high. I would sit in this car sweating like a pig in a slaughterhouse. I dared not roll the window glass down lest my "home" be flooded.

I made more money in a week by staying in the parking lot of the restaurant. Anytime someone called in sick, I was right there. All the manager had to do was ask someone to knock on my window. Sometimes they would startle me with a bang on the window as I slept. I was always ready.

I loved my car because I could go wherever I wanted to go. I no longer had to worry about bothering my roommate to take me to work. It was true I had had fun riding with him. People always knew when we were approaching. His car emitted smoke from the exhaust that would envelop everything behind it. Its thunderous roar awakened everyone in the neighborhood.

That didn't matter at all. I appreciated him very much. But now I could drive to school without having to wait for someone to drop me off or spend hours sitting on a bus to downtown. It took between thirty and forty-five minutes to drive in a friend's car to the downtown campus of the University of Houston. In a bus, the journey took over two hours. I loved my "new" car. I no longer had to wake up in the wee hours of the morning to catch a bus to make it to my eight o'clock class after having worked from five o'clock the previous evening till about three thirty in the morning.

At school, I met more students from my home country, Nigeria, and those from other African countries. I quickly found out that I was not alone in this experience. Each of them had a similar experience to share.

One of my friends, Uche, worked as a paper boy for a local newspaper company. Very early in the morning, he went to the warehouse, where he folded the papers, rubber-banded them, and packed them in his boss's car. They then drove from door to door, throwing those papers to each house on their assigned route. His boss did the driving as Uche tossed the papers onto the driveways. Uche went home afterward to get ready for school.

Countless stories were told. There was a man who had been a medical doctor in his home country. He sold his medical practice to come to America. He left his family at home. When he arrived in Houston, he found out that he could not practice medicine without an American medical license. He could not work anywhere in the capacity of a medical doctor because the American medical system would not tolerate any foreign-trained doctor who had not proven himself or herself by passing a litany of required examinations.

He tried everything he could to pass those examinations, but when he discovered that he was running out of money, he had no other choice but to work as a "sitter" or a psychiatric technician in one hospital or another to make ends meet. He even worked as a nurse's aide, cleaning patients and washing their soiled laundry. He became so frustrated that he began to contemplate going back home, but it was too late. He had sold his practice. He had sold everything he had. Returning home would spell disaster. He had been displaced. So he killed that idea and decided to tough it out.

I was washing the windows of the restaurant one day when a man in his late thirties walked into the restaurant.

"Customer service!" I called out.

"Welcome to Taco Bell. May I take your order?" a girl said, walking toward the front line.

"Is the manager here?" the man inquired.

"Yes, just a minute," the girl responded. She walked to the back office. Seconds later, she reemerged with the store manager. "This gentleman wants to see you," she said.

"Hi, I'm the manager. How may I help you?"

"Are you hiring?" the man asked almost timidly.

"Sure. Let me get you an application," the manager responded, walking back to his office. Moments later, he came back with an application form. "Fill this out and give it back to me," he said, handing the application to the man.

As the man sat down in the lobby to complete the application, I walked up and greeted him. "How are you doing?"

"I'm good, and how are you?" he responded.

"Are you from Nigeria?" I asked.

The man hesitated to respond, but it was obvious to me that he was from Nigeria. He seemed insecure about revealing his nationality, but the tribal marks on his face gave him away, as far as I was concerned. I could have been wrong. Such marks were not peculiar to Nigerians.

"I'm from West Africa," he responded.

"I know you are from West Africa, but from which country in West Africa?"

"Where are you from?" the man inquired. He still hadn't answered my question.

"I am from Nigeria," I told him.

"Well, I am from Nigeria too," he finally admitted. "I'm looking for a job. Maybe you can help me talk to the manager."

His name was Ishiola. From the way he presented his argument, I immediately noticed that he was intelligent and very sharp. His English was impeccable.

I was right. Ishiola had been an established lawyer in Nigeria. He had given up his law practice to come to America, hoping that he would find a decent law firm to work for. For over a year, he had worked as a pizza delivery boy. His father had died of a heart attack, and he wasn't able to travel home. He had come to Taco Bell seeking a second job in an attempt to make ends meet.

Ishiola's situation was not unique. There were many others who had the desire to emigrate to the United States to seek a better life. This desire was fueled and intensified by the poor economic and social conditions and the unfortunate characteristics that had undermined many nations' weak democratic bases. There were others who were pulled by the American dream and those who were seized by curiosity.

Like Ishiola, many left behind their parents, wives, children, businesses, or jobs. They came with extravagant dreams and lavish expectations. Some came, like I did, to experience the "stuff of overblown hopes" (Takaki, 1993).

Ishiola told me about his friend Tunde, who was also a lawyer in Nigeria. When Tunde was in Nigeria, he thought that his cousins in America were stingy and wicked and didn't care about anybody at home, including their parents, because the emigrants did not send home money on demand. He was one of those who thought that money grew on trees in America, and anybody who couldn't make it in America could not make it anywhere in life. Tunde boasted about how he would make things happen if he had a chance to go to America.

Then Tunde won the immigration lottery and decided to abandon his successful legal practice to pursue his lofty dream of making it big in America. He left his wife and children behind with the hope of getting things together in America before they joined him.

Well, when he came, he squatted with his cousin for about six months, trying to secure employment with a law firm or perhaps open his own law firm. He dressed up every morning in his suit and briefcase and went from one law firm to another. Some looked through his credentials, and others just told him they had no position available. He returned home every day frustrated and worn.

His cousin drove an ice cream truck from neighborhood to neighborhood and sometimes parked his truck to attend classes at the university. He offered to rent an ice cream truck for Tunde so he could at least have something to do. Tunde thought it was ridiculous, and he accused his cousin of insult. His cousin had had enough. He asked Tunde to either find a job to help pay the bills or find somewhere else to stay.

Tunde's first job was at McDonald's, where he was hired to wash dishes and clean the floors. After few weeks of this "rubbish," as he called it, he decided to do something about the situation. His cousin came home one morning and found his body dangling from a ceiling fan.

There was no money to send Tunde's body home, so a wake-keeping was organized, and members of his community were kind enough to donate money. Sufficient funds were raised, and his body was flown home and buried.

Ishiola completed the Taco Bell application and turned it in. The manager interviewed him instantly, and he was hired to work the night shift. I also worked the night shift, and Ishiola and I eventually became friends.

I got off from work earlier than normal one evening. I had been invited to a dinner party by a classmate, Deje, who lived with his uncle. Deje had told me that his uncle's wife had included farina with *egusi* and *ogbono* soup on the menu for the evening, in addition to other Nigerian dishes.

I could not wait. I had not had home-cooked soup since I came to America. I had settled for tacos and burritos and nachos. Once in a while, for a taste of something different, I called a nearby restaurant to trade tacos for their food. The closest I came to enjoying foo-foo was when I mixed okra and sardine together. It was good too. My friends and I usually made do with masa trigo and okra soup mixed with stew, popularly known as *ewedu*. The density of the farina would usually knock us off to sleep.

Deje's uncle, Uncle Oji as he was known, and his family had relocated to the United States from Nigeria. Uncle Oji had been a professor of chemistry at one of the universities in Nigeria. He had won the immigration lottery and brought his family of three girls and a boy along. Nneka was sixteen, Nkechi fourteen, Chioma twelve, and Chima eight.

Uncle Oji had sought employment at several universities but to no avail. They required him to have a minimum of three years of public school teaching experience in America. When he saw that he was not succeeding in getting the job he thought he was qualified for, and funds were running out, he resorted to cab driving.

His wife, Auntie Chinelo, who had also been a teacher at a high school in Nigeria, discovered that she was not qualified to teach even at a primary school in America. She had to have a bachelor's degree and a teaching certificate to qualify. She found a job at a day care center.

After several months at this menial job, earning little or no money, Auntie Chinelo decided to go to nursing school. Nursing was a profession she had despised while she was in Nigeria, but circumstances had changed her thinking. For her to survive in America, she had to find a profession that would make life better for her family. She now saw nursing as the quickest means of making a decent living.

Auntie Chinelo had a very funny way of waking her children up, especially on weekends. "It is nine o'clock on Saturday morning, and you all are still sleeping. Go anywhere and check; all your mates are up and have cleaned their houses, and you are still lying down here sleeping. Get up right now or I'll slap you out of the bed. Nonsense!"

The girls would scamper out of bed with sleepy eyes.

"Nneka, come here!" Auntie Chinelo would yell. "So you are frowning because I woke you up, ah? You, Nkechi, so you are a big woman now that you can't say good morning? *Ngwa*, go and start cleaning up right now. Chioma-a-a-a! Chioma-a-a-a! Come on, get up! Didn't you hear my voice? *Oya*, go and find something to do right now. You can make breakfast. You think you are too young to cook? Ogechi is your mate. She cooks everything, and she makes all As in school! When you get married, you will call me to come and cook for you and your husband. Nonsense!"

"What does that have to do with anything?" Chioma might murmur.

"Come here! What did you just say? Oh, you are talking back to me? Are you talking back?" Auntie Chinelo would yell, looking for a stick.

Meanwhile, Chioma would have disappeared. The other girls dared not say a word! Of course, Auntie's questions needed no answers, and the girls knew that. All they had to do was get busy, and they did.

Months passed. Auntie Chinelo completed her nursing program, and this dinner was her graduation party. It turned out to be more than just a dinner party. There was music, dancing, and different types of food, including moi-moi and fried plantain. I hadn't seen such food since I came to America. For the first time in years, I enjoyed home cooking.

During the party, Auntie Chinelo thanked her husband for being so generous, kind, and patient, and for paying her way through nursing school. "Such husbands are rare," she concluded. Everyone applauded.

Auntie Chinelo was right. Such husbands were rare. However, after the dust settled, Auntie Chinelo passed her board exams and found a job at a nearby hospital. For several months, things seemed to be going great. Then one day, Uncle Oji came home from making his last round, tired and worn. There was no food for him to eat, and Auntie Chinelo had gone to bed for the night.

I had just opened the restaurant lobby when a customer walked in. "Are y'all open?" he inquired.

"Sure," I responded, walking toward the cash register. "May I take your order?"

"Yes. Let me have two tacos, one tostada, and one burrito supreme. That's it," he said.

"Would you like something to drink with that?" I asked politely.

"Yes," he said. "Make it a medium Coke."

"Would you accept Pepsi instead?" I asked.

"Make it Dr Pepper," he responded.

I rang up the order. In a few seconds, the order was ready. "Enjoy your meal," I said, handing the customer his tray.

I enjoyed my new position as the point-of-sale person. The new assignment included customer service, stocking the condiments, making sure the windows were clean, checking the lobby trash bins to be sure they were not overflowing, and keeping the floor clean. Once in a while, when there were no customers to attend to and when all the frontline items were taken care of, I washed dishes, cleaned the sink, or set up the Hobart machine to shred lettuce and cheese.

Another customer walked in, and I washed my hands and came to the front line. "May I take your order?"

"No, thank you," he responded. "I'm looking for Ishiola. Does he work here?"

"Yes," I responded, "but he is off today."

"Do you know when next he will be working?"

"Ummm, I really don't know," I responded hesitantly.

"Okay," he said and turned.

"Is there a message for him?" I called after him.

"No, that's all right," the man said, walking away.

I knew things were not right, but I didn't know what the problem was. Ishiola had not come to work for the past four days. He had called in sick most of the time, and that was quite unlike him. I called Ishiola's number, but the phone had been disconnected.

The truth was that Ishiola had gotten himself entangled with the wrong people. He badly needed money to send home. Since he had learned that his father had had a stroke, he hadn't gotten any opportunity to visit home; neither had he sent money. His wife had called and threatened to go back to her parents with the children if he didn't bring them over to America. The little money he made working at Pizza Hut and Taco Bell was not even enough to cover his rent and other bills. He had become frustrated and stressed out, and looked for a quicker means of making money.

I finally realized that the man who had come looking for him was an FBI agent. Ishiola had gotten involved in credit card fraud. The FBI had gone to his apartment, and he wasn't there, so they came to look for him at work. Ishiola had packed up his belongings and fled back to Nigeria.

I called Deje to tell him what had happened. Deje did not answer the phone. No one answered that number. Later that evening, I went to school, but Deje wasn't in class. He knew there was an exam that day. His uncle usually dropped him off in his yellow cab. I wondered what had happened.

After class, I hurried to Deje's apartment to find out if all was well. No one was there. The apartment was empty. They had moved out, and I didn't have a clue where they had moved to. I went home that day very sad. That apartment had been where I ate my first homemade soup and enjoyed the best time of my life.

Uncle Oji and Auntie Chinelo had separated. Uncle Oji found out that Auntie Chinelo had opened her own bank account and on several occasions had sent money home to her parents without telling Uncle Oji. A letter came in the mail from Auntie Chinelo's mother, thanking Uncle Oji for sending her such a huge sum of money. When Uncle Oji confronted his wife about it, she told Uncle Oji that it was her money, and she could do whatever she wanted to do with it. After all, for the past two years, she had been the only one taking care of the family.

"What are you talking about, 'your money'?" Uncle Oji yelled. "After all, it was my sweat. After I worked my bottom off training you in nursing school, now you have the guts to talk about 'your money.'"

"For the past two years, I have done everything for this family, including feeding you and paying the children's day care fees. Haven't you gotten your sweat back?" Auntie Chinelo retorted.

Uncle Oji was furious. He slapped Auntie Chinelo across the mouth to shut her up. Auntie Chinelo called the police, and they took Uncle Oji to jail. He called his friends who bailed him out. Before Uncle Oji could come back from jail, Auntie Chinelo moved out with their two younger children.

Meanwhile, Deje had gone to stay temporarily with Emeka, a friend he met during Auntie Chinelo's graduation party.

It wasn't long before Auntie Chinelo brought her mother over to care for her children while she worked. She would work all available shifts in addition to her regular shift. She basically lived in the hospital. She even had a weekend job at a different hospital. She soon bought a big house and a Lexus. When she had her housewarming party, the neighborhood streets were flooded with cars—big cars. Most of her guests were nurses, and most of them were divorced or separated. I wondered if they had an association.

"I make the big bucks!" That was their slogan. Auntie Chinelo even began to build a house in Nigeria for her parents. Her mother didn't ask her about her husband, and Auntie Chinelo didn't discuss what had transpired. She was making a lot of money, and that was all Auntie Chinelo or her mother cared about.

One day, as her mother was getting the children ready to catch the school bus, the telephone rang. It was the hospital where Auntie Chinelo worked. One of her daughters picked up the phone, thinking that it was her mother. Chinelo's coworker was calling to inform Chinelo's mother that Chinelo had had a massive heart attack. Before her mother could get to the hospital, Chinelo had died. She had collapsed during shift change. They tried to resuscitate her, but to no avail.

Auntie Chinelo's wake and funeral service were awesome experiences. Uncle Oji claimed his wife from the hospital, made the funeral arrangements, and arranged the wake. Uncle Oji's friends rallied around him as a committee of friends and gave him support. Auntie Chinelo's body was finally flown home and buried. Her mother returned to Nigeria. Uncle Oji kept his children and the car and the house. He eventually sold the house, but he kept the car since it was already paid for.

I hadn't yet received my bachelor's degree when my wife came from Nigeria to join me. I had met her while I was at home. Her older brother, whom I called Silencer, was my very good friend and roommate while we were in Port-Harcourt. All through the time we were together, I didn't know he had a sister. He never brought her up in a conversation, and he never showed her picture publicly, especially where his male friends were.

I had other friends who came from the same village as Silencer, and they invited all of us to their village, Umuahia, to celebrate Christmas together. It was there that I found out my very good friend and roommate of many years had a sister. She was his only sister and younger, and I could understand why he was so overly protective. She was so beautiful that I was ready to risk my friendship with Silencer to be with her.

As we young men were walking out in group to visit other friends across the road, I saw her sitting alone on the pavement. I withdrew from the crowd. I saw that Silencer was busy with the group and the good time. I quickly made my move. I went to her to make my demands. I knew I didn't have time to dance around. I wasn't sure what her reaction was going to be, but I knew I was at an advantage because she knew I was her brother's friend.

Her smile was welcoming as I approached.

"I'm Silencer's friend," I said as a form of introduction.

"I know you," she said. "I have seen you several times."

"Wow! So you know my name, then?" I inquired.

"Yes! Darlington," she responded with utter certainty.

I felt a warm sensation run through my body, from my head to my toes. I lost my train of thought right away. "So you know me very well!" I exclaimed, for lack of anything better to say.

She nodded her head, still smiling.

Immediately, I put in my request. "Can you give me your address?"

"Sure," she said. "Let me get a paper and a pen."

Moments later she returned with a piece of paper. She handed it to me, and I glanced at it with sentimental eyes. I quickly tore off part of the paper, wrote down my address, and gave it to her. We exchanged pleasantries.

I didn't realize that Silencer had noticed that I was not with the group. He had seen his sister sitting out there when the group was passing through. His hunch told him that I must be with his sister. As soon as I turned around to go back to the group, I ran into Silencer.

"Ole boy, give me that paper!" he demanded.

"Which paper?" I asked.

"Just give me the piece of paper. You think I didn't see you? Just give it to me."

I wasn't sure if he had seen me or not, but since he mentioned the piece of paper, I believed he knew what he was talking about. I handed the paper to him. He immediately tossed it in his mouth and chewed, just to make sure that nothing of it was decipherable. He was a good protective sergeant, but what he didn't know was that I had already memorized the address.

My wife (well, we weren't married then) was still in high school when I left for the United States. No day went by without her receiving a letter from me. I would write many of them and put them in the mailbox at the same time. I was told that the school mail carrier would sort out her letters first. He bundled them together and tied them up so that he won't have to call each letter out individually. Some days, she would receive six letters or more. Her friends created a nickname for her, Pessylington, which was a combination of my name and her name.

As soon as she graduated from high school, I sent word to my father that I had found a girl I would like to marry. My father hadn't met her. In our culture, we took filial piety, or respect for parents and elders, very seriously. We dared not take our female friends to our parents' house. We did not want our parents, or any adult for that matter, to catch us standing with a girl on the street, let alone at home. So my father hadn't met her. I gave him directions to her parents' village, and my father went to check her out.

I didn't know what his response would be after the visit, but I was waiting anxiously for his approval. I couldn't wait to call home to find out what his opinion was. When I called, my father told me that they had just returned from Umuahia. He went with other elders because, as the Igbo say, "A snake seen by one person soon becomes a python."

"We have just returned," he said.

"Okay …" I said, waiting.

He still wasn't saying what I wanted to hear, so I demanded, "What do you think?"

"*Nwa m* (my son), you know a good thing when you see one!"

Boy, I was just as excited as I was when he first told me that I would go to America and become a doctor and a professor. I thanked him immensely, and from that point, the marriage process began.

The "question askers" had done their job, and everything was fine. The marriage had been cleared to proceed, so my family and almost the entire village went to our would-be in-laws' house. Her family presented my family fresh palm wine and kola nut. After they had eaten, my father cleared his throat and formally told her family his reason for coming.

Agwala, kwenu!
Echiele, kwenu!
Otampa, kwenu!
Isuikwuato, kwezuonu!

After each greeting, the audience responded with a resounding "Yaah!"

"The lioness we were chasing ran into your house, and we have come in pursuit," my father said, bunching his huge dashiki to the right and to the left in a blatant expression of pride.

159

Everyone laughed and clapped in frenzy. They understood the saying. My wife's father had died, so her oldest brother, Ogbulefu, who had assumed the role of the head of the family unit, stood up, cleared his throat, and bellowed:

> *Adindu, kwenu!*
> *Umuohu, kwenu!*
> *Ndume, kwenu!*
> *Ibeku, kwezuonu!*

"You are all welcome. That lioness belongs to me."

He asked one of the boys to call his baby sister. There was silence. Moments later, she appeared, dressed in a uniquely tied wrapper, short at the knees and through the underarm, covering her torso and thighs and leaving the rest of the body bare. Beaded necklaces adorned her neck. She had earrings and bracelets to match. There were also beads of orange and black *jigida* around her waist, dropping down to her buttocks. Her hair was intricately braided in cornrows.

Shouts of excitement heralded her entrance. She walked straight to her big brother and knelt on one knee in respect.

"*Bilie* (stand up)," he said, gesturing. "Do you know who the visitors are?"

"Yes," she said, blushing.

"Very good," her brother said. "Now, go back into the house, and we will call you when we need you."

My wife bowed in obeisance and went back inside, and immediately the traditional bride pricing or dowry negotiation began.

It was the tradition among my people that a prospective husband was expected to give a certain amount of money and goods before a marriage was agreed. This age-old tradition was revered as a symbol of sincerity and good faith that brought two families together—the bride's and groom's families and, in fact, the entire kinship network of the village. Some outsiders have interpreted the bride price as a means to enrich the bride's family, but the truth is that a dowry created a bond between the families as well as the bride and groom.

As soon as an agreement was reached and everyone was in accord, they sent someone to bring out my wife again.

"Show me and all your people who are gathered here today who the chief hunter is," her brother requested.

He filled up a little calabash of palm wine, gave it to her, and asked her to give it to the "chief hunter." She took the calabash, walked through the crowd for a while, and handed it to my father. Everyone cheered.

My father thanked our in-laws for giving him their lovely daughter in marriage. "I have always dreamed of a wife this beautiful and from such a great family for my son. I thank God for giving you the blessing and favor to raise the woman of my dreams," my father said. He also thanked everyone who had come to support him.

There was plenty to eat and drink. Different groups performed their cultural dances. The ceremony went into the wee hours of the morning.

My wife finally came to America, and we began our life together. She started college, and I was still taking classes too. She was here when I received my bachelor's degree. She was here when I received my master's degree. She was here when I received my doctorate. She received her degrees in nursing while at the same time raising our four beautiful children.

After my bachelor's degree, I wanted to continue my passion for teaching, but friends told me that it would be difficult in America because of my accent. They tried to talk me out of it, saying that the students would not understand me.

I heeded their advice for a moment. I applied to law school, which was another interest of mine, and gained admission. I knew I would perhaps make more money as a lawyer, but I still felt some emptiness inside of me. I wanted to pursue my original passion. I put a foot forward, turned down the law school admission, and applied to become a teacher.

It worked! I stirred up the gift in me and DARE-d myself to unleash. I arose, took off my shoes, and continued to PUSH. I took the STEP, unleashed my CASH, connected, put a *fruit* forward, and the rest is history.

I received an outstanding teacher award. Then I was named teacher of the year. Then I became an instructional coordinator. Then I was appointed a member of the principals' academy.

I went on to become a professor. Then I received a dean's faculty excellence award. Then I became a member of the faculty senate. Then I became acting department head.

Finally, I became an adult Christian education teacher at my church, and then the adult Christian education coordinator.

Bill Gates (I hope you know of him) went to college to study law. His gift pulled him in a different direction. He put a foot forward and followed his passion, his heart. He unleashed his potential, and the rest is history.

Not everyone can be a lawyer, a doctor, a professor, an engineer, a pastor, or a prophet, but everyone has a special gift, and everyone can become something. What is your gift? What is your passion?

Look into your BACKPACK. Prepare yourself; understand who you are. Unlock that PADLOCK. Unleash your potential. Put a foot forward, and take that STEP. The rest will become history!

References

Conwell, Russell, and Robert Shackleton. *Acres of Diamonds*. Stilwell, KS: Digireads, 2008.

Ortberg, John. *If You Want to Walk on Water, You've Got to Get Out of the Boat*. Grand Rapids, MI: Zondervan, 2001.

Takaki, Ronald. *A Different Mirror: A History of Multicultural America*. Boston: Little, Brown and Company, 1993.